THE WORTH OF RELIGIOUS TRUTH-CLAIMS

A Case for Religious Education

Tan Tai Wei

UNIVERSITY
PRESS OF
AMERICA

TO THE MEMORY OF TAN KENG CHENG, MY FATHER,
WHO DIED ON 13TH OCTOBER 1980 AT 75

Totally paralysed and at the point of death at 40,
he had recovered only to spend 35 years a cripple at home,
mostly bedridden and in constant discomfort, the last 2
years again in total paralysis, this time speechless. However, those very circumstances, that seemed ultimately so
callous and meaningless, were in part the occasion for his
spontaneous recovery from 'certain' death that coincided
exactly with prayers, the hearing of a 'voice', and the
seeing of a 'vision'. His personal conviction that a
'miracle' had happened was a major factor sustaining him
and his family thereafter. And some of   the sufferings
he and his family underwent can no doubt be explained in
terms of a deepening of their moral and religious convic-
tions.

His life therefore exemplified, in some measure,
the observations of this monograph concerning its two key
points of contention, i.e. the conceivability of a solution of the problem of pain based on partial solutions as
viewed from the human perspective, mooted in Part One; and
the intelligibility and possibility of identifying
'miracles' based on such coincidence of events as exemplified above, discussed in Part Two. It is thus appropriate to dedicate this book to his memory.

iii

ACKNOWLEDGEMENTS

I have in writing this monograph made extensive use of material originally published as five papers. Section II of Part One appeared as 'Extraterrestrial Persons and Religious Tradition' in Sophia Vol X, No.2, 1971. Pages 64-66 and pages 70-72 of Section III, Part One occurred as parts of 'The Question of a Cosmomorphic Utopia', The Personalist, Vol. LV, No.4, 1974. Section I of Part Two appeared as 'Some Purported Grounds for Theism', Sophia, Vol. XV, No. 2, 1976. Most of Section II (i) of Part Two was published as 'Recent Discussions On Miracles' Sophia Vol. XI, No. 3, 1972, whereas most of Section II (ii) appeared as 'Supernatural Events and a Case for Theism' The Philosophical Journal Vol. XII, No. 1, 1975. I am grateful to the editors and publishers of the journals for permission to use the material here.

Professor Roland Puccetti read a draft of the paper 'Extraterrestrial Persons and Religious Tradition' and his comments on it helped me to anticipate a couple of objections to the argument. I have also, in writing 'Recent Discussions On Miracles', benefitted from comments from Professor Puccetti, Mr C.L. Ten, and Professor M.J. Charlesworth. It is therefore right that I thank these gentlemen again here, since the same material has been used.

I should also thank Chwee Hoon and Wei Ming, my wife and son, for having endured the times when, because of the concerns of this book, I could accede to their rights to my attention with only listless stares. One major setback of philosophic research is that you can't leave your laboratory and come home!

Tan Tai Wei,
Institute of Education,
Singapore; April, 1981.

CONTENTS

INTRODUCTION

AGAINST SECULARISM IN EDUCATION

This essay argues, on the assumption that education has <u>inter alia</u> to be liberal, i.e. it should aim at the promotion of knowledge and understanding in depth and breadth for its intrinsic worth*, that a truly liberal education cannot afford to ignore traditional religious truth-claims in the manner, as will be explained, of the prevailing secularism (at least among curriculum theorists and philosophers), since there are good reasons to teach them as viable claims to knowledge. Now, as we will elaborate, there is no dispute about the rightful place in a liberal education of the established branches of <u>secular</u> knowledge; therefore our contention would, in remedying the contemporary lack arising from the unwarranted secularistic presumptions, suffice to somewhat complete the picture of what the content of a liberal education should be in terms of a comprehensive coverage of established and possible knowledge-claims.

I argue that the widespread contemporary disregard for, or mere lip service paid in curriculum theory and practice to, instruction in traditional religions that make truth-claims to a transcendent God and/or a transnatural and transhuman reality, being or beings (in what follows, I shall call such religious assertions 'orthodox'), is unduly presumptuous. This secularism, assumed or even actively advocated by educational theorists and philosophers, if not accepted universally by educational practitioners, is especially disturbing occurring as it does at the present state of educational theorising where much attention is being given to justifying and structuring the place in education of the acknowledged secular branches of knowledge.

---

*   I have elsewhere argued, <u>pace</u> R.S. Peters (Peters, 1966, especially Chap. 5; 1973a), that since education is the upbringing of man, it must include the promotion of his knowledge and understanding ideally in all depth and breadth for its intrinsic worth. For the form of life that defines man as man is the rational life, and rationality is inseparable from knowledge and understanding. (See Tan, 1978, especially Chap. 6)

We show that there are rational considerations that do put the truth-claims of orthodox religions at least on par with the interesting and deserving hypotheses to truth of secular knowledge, giving them the same importance in liberal education, concerned, as it is, with all possibilities of knowledge and understanding.

Although disputes have occurred in contemporary analytic educational philosophy and in philosophy in general about the logical structure and possible logical divisions of distinct types of truths (understanding of which would be necessary for determining the nature and scope of a liberal education),* no one has doubted the epistemological value of all the secular areas of enquiry and the need to include them in a liberal curriculum in some arrangement. However, at the same time, the orthodox religious claims to truth, as we shall see, are mostly quickly reduced to and identified with one or two areas of secular knowledge in discussions on the import of religious education, with no serious attempt made even at undermining the truth-claims of religious orthodoxy. The presumption seems to be that mainstream philosophy has already conclusively rebutted religious orthodoxy and so educational philosophers may simply proceed to give religions the only sort of sense they can have and write on 'religious education' in such reduced senses of religion. Thus both Peters and another prominent current educational philosopher seem to regard the core of religions to be in the emotions and attitudes with regard to the ultimate questions traditional religions ask rather than the answers they have tried to give. (Peters, 1973b, lecture four; Wilson, 1971) The latter therefore they ignore, regarding religious education merely in terms of the cognitive appreciation of what would be appropriate 'this-worldly' objects of such emotions as awe and reverence. Religious truth-claims are thus reduced in import and purport to an emotionally involved kind of ultimate socio-anthropological perspective of the human condition. In the philosophy of religion proper, Braithwaite in a well-known essay (Braithwaite, 1971) identified religion with morality - an agapeistic way of life in the case of Christianity - and took the transnatural referents of religions

---

* See Hirst, 1974, especially pp. 30-53 for his 'forms of knowledge' thesis, pp. 54-68 for his critique of the 'realms of meaning' thesis of P.H. Phenix (Phenix, 1964), and pp. 54-100 for his defence against attacks on his own thesis.

to be mere stories told to psychologically reinforce the moral stance. To Miles (Miles, 1959) religion is 'silence qualified by parables', a reductionism not unlike Peters' and Wilson's. Hare (1971) has said that ultimately religion is the evincing of 'a blik' - an ultimate unprovable and indisprovable attitude to things, like belief in the regularity of nature or the lunatic's deranged view of things. In the case of religion, the 'blik' would of courses be inextricably bound up with adopting a moral stance. Among such reductionistic 'religious' views, it is Wittgensteinian philosophers, prominently Peter Winch and D.Z. Phillips (see, for instance Winch, 1977; Phillips, 1965), who have boldy asserted that if traditional religious language is properly understood, then it is clear that to conceive of the transcendent as being referred to in religious discourse is to miss the real point of religious language. Understanding a religion is merely understanding and being initiated into a socio-anthropological perspective as presupposed in the cultural group-practice concerned, wherein certain models or 'pictures', i.e. the preternatural referents of the religion, have only a 'this-worldly' practical function. Now all such reductionisms thrive, I think, basically on the common empiricist presumption that references to the preternatural and transcendent are meaningless because they are unstatable empirically, and thus lack a genuine use in human language. Only on this presumption would it be even sensible to claim an unfamiliar and recently conceived sense to have been the real meaning of traditional religions all along. For if the transcendent referents were senseless, then, since religious language has had a significant use, or could continue to have such a use with some basic semantic modifications, the reductions recommended would at least enable 'religion' to retain some such sense. (It follows from this that if we succeed in showing this presumption premature, we will already have enough to justify ignoring the novel views).

It is true that in secular epistemology, such reduction of one kind or area of knowledge to another has also been attempted. Thus there have been attempts to reduce the moral 'ought' to other 'oughts' or to 'is', and knowledge of minds in terms of intention, belief and reason has been argued by some determinists or materialists to be reducible to the kind of knowledge in terms of cause-and-effect whose paradigm is the physical sciences. These reductionistic moves are at least extraordinary and stand in need of an adequate defence which has yet, I think, to be given. Anyhow, their truth would by no means affect the historical identify of the knowledge concerned to the point of unrecognisability, in the way the said reduction of religions would affect relgions, at any rate for most ordinary, practical worshippers within the historical religious traditions. For instance, compatibilists in the freewill-determinism debate stress that even within a totally materialistic, determinist universe, belief, intention, rationality and choice would still retain their ordinary meanings in the context of day-to-day discourse in the distinction that would still persist between, say, 'our jumping out of the window', and 'our being thrown out of the window'. (See Flew, 1973, p. 239). The metaphysical deterministic view would only affect the macro-significance of those actions and beliefs. It is not that the latter is not of grave import; it is just that the outcome would be recognisably an interpretation of what we ordinarily regard as mental events. There has been a long tradition of debate in which both libertarian and deterministic views are recognisably attempted accounts of mental events. It is the same with morality. Whether, say, the is-ought distinction can be sustained or not would have little effect with regard to the historical continuity and recognisability of either account as an interpretation of moral discourse. Ethical naturalism, for instance, is a historically recognised moral theory. Now these reductionistic attempts would, of course, affect the sort of logical demarcations of truth-enquiry into 'forms of knowledge' or 'realms of meaning' attempted by Hirst and Phenix respectively (see footnote above). But however mind and morality are characterised, that would not alter the common agreement that there are these two areas of knowledge-concern which liberal education must promote and transmit. In the case of religion, however, the common assumption is that unless a reductionistic interpretation is given to religious assertions, a liberal education ought not to transmit them if indoctrination is to be avoided. And that the reduction of religions would render the new accounts unrecognisable as religion, unlike in the secular examples given above, is evident in that those recent philosophical theologians who claim to be believers but who say such things as that 'God is dead' have been called 'modernists' or other recently concocted but internally strained terms like 'Christian atheists' or 'religious secularists' , whereas ethical naturalism and materialism seem as ancient as philosophy.

Therefore as a corrective to what I consider to be an unwarranted bias against religious orthodoxy in current conceptions of the nature and scope of liberal education and knowledge, I concern myself exclusively with upholding the epistemological value of 'religious knowledge'. After all, as we shall mention, if orthodox religious claims were true, the ultimate epistemological perspective for viewing the secular areas of knowledge would be drastically altered and their horizons unimaginably widened. And, of course, religious truths would have taken on permanent or 'eternal' educational significaance that many this-worldly truth-enquiries would lack.

I shall have to aim at some originality and relative comprehensiveness. For while in general epistemology, discussions adequately endorse the current presumption in favour of the status accorded the secular areas of knowledge, in the philosophy of religion, even among writers sympathetic to orthodox religion, things are very much still at sea (as we shall illustrate), with little definitive guidance for the educational philosopher. And the occasional contemporary educational philosopher who has entertained the possibility of orthodox religions having educational import has left it only as a conditional possibility without actually coming to grips with the subject matter of religious truth-claims themselves and settling the issue in some substantive and definitive manner. Thus Hirst, in raising the possibility of orthodox religions comprising yet another form of knowledge to add to his list of secular purportedly distinct and irreducible forms, merely remarks: 'Religious claims in their traditional forms certainly make use of concepts which, it is now maintained, are irreducible in character; whether or not there are objective grounds for what is asserted is a matter on which much more has yet to be said. The case would certainly seem to be one that cannot be simply dismissed.' (Peters, Hirst, 1970, p. 64).

The upshot, in terms of my contribution to the contemporary philosophic discussions of educational issues pertaining to the thesis, therefore, is the bridging of a substantive analytical and justificatory gap in current thinking on liberal education and the extent of knowledge or possible knowledge that this should transmit. But of course, the essay is also a contribution on fundamental issues in the philosophy of religion itself.

PART ONE

RELIGIOUS TRUTH-CLAIMS AND INTELLIGIBILITY

I PREAMBLE

Now it is not always necessary, for a case for the inclusion of instructional matter in the liberal education curriculum, for it to have been established truth. For there should also be a place in liberal education for the transmission of genuine and interesting hypotheses and initially plausible insights and conjectures. The exclusion of these could mean the stifling of the development of knowledge at its roots, for the next generation of mankind would then be deprived of the opportunity to test them and hopefully thereby to expand the frontiers of the knowledge concerned. And with regard to possible religious knowledge, which if true would, we said (Cf. p.xiii) alter the entire perspective within which all the secular areas of knowledge would have ultimately to be understood, the more urgency there would be to pass on such initial insights. It would seem therefore that if we could establish religious truth-claims as serious and initially plausible contenders to truth, we would already have a case for religious education conceived as the understanding of the nature and grounds of religious insights, and the sort of tests they would have to undergo in order to become established truths. It may be objected that truth-hypotheses and the like can only arise in the context within established forms of knowledge, whereas in the case of religion, whether there exists a religious kind of knowledge at all, and even what might be the nature of the truth-tests that would be appropriate for religion, are themselves questions at issue. But this objection may be allayed by observing that there would be the general norms of rationality that all established and putative kinds of knowledge must mutatis mutandis acknowledge, whose truth criteria all established knowledge must have begun by satisfying. And the various forms of knowledge being already established, they surely comprise the context or rational backdrop against which the truth-claims of putative new sorts of knowledge would initially be judged. Some procedure such as just outlined must be in order for the validating of new sorts of truths: how else would new kinds of knowledge be conceivable?

I want therefore in this and the next part of the monograph to merely provide grounds to maintain that the truth-claims of religion should be taken as serious and deserving contenders to truth. This limited task will already have far-reaching significance considering the present climate of thinking about religion and religious education mentioned in our Introduction.

Now two necessary and when taken together sufficient criteria will have to be met before religious truth-claims may be advanced as serious and viable contenders to truth. Firstly, they must make sufficient sense in terms of the public language of human discourse for them to be regarded as intelligible. This is an obvious point, except that it has not usually been noticed that it is implied in the central theistic doctrine of divine revelation. Revelation presupposes the possibility and at least some success of divine communication with men, and this means that religious truths so revealed must make at least the minimal sense in terms of human experience and language necessary for the revelatory communication. But of course, because religion, in the orthodox interpretation of it, asserts truths of a transnatural and transhuman kind (which by definition concerns fundamentally matters beyond the ken of natural human experience), we should, while insisting on this criterion of minimal intelligibility, not enforce ordinary language semantic strictures on religious language to such an extent as to rule out what should really be expected of religious utterances, i.e. fundamental departures from ordinary language meanings whilst maintaining the minimal intelligibility just specified. To do so would be not at all to begin the enquiry into the validity of <u>religious</u> truth-claims. (Divine revelation is a central religious tenet. If religion were claimed to be entirely the product of the human mind, then it might be plausible to say that since man could only give it the sense he could make of it, purported religious meanings that depart from the ordinary and natural just could not be meaningful. Even this would be arguable, for surely we cannot rule out at the start the possibility that intimations of a transnatural realm of being may be had by the receptive human mind, say, in a Wordsworthian contemplation of nature). Exactly how, in the light of the above observations, religious truth-claims will have to meet the

criterion of minimal sensibility is a matter that has
to be decided in the actual consideration of particular
truth-claims.

The second criterion is that there must be sufficient initial indications or evidences in favour of
religious truth-claims that would distinguish them
from such other intelligible truth-claims as can be
concocted, but which we could take seriously only on
pains of risking having to consider every other possible truth-claim imaginable. Since the class of possible sensible religious truth-assertions can be assumed
to be far larger than the class of such truth-claims
that deserve consideration, it is quite right that not
any sensible truth-assertion but only those that show
initial evidential promise through meeting our second
criterion be admissible. But here again, exactly what
counts as meeting this criterion is a substantive question that cannot be answered in general, and will have
to depend on the specific evidences and arguments
advanced and how convincing they can be shown to be
vis-a-vis the type of truth they purport to uphold.

We have therefore to argue that religious
truth-claims do meet the above two criteria. Now, I
shall discuss this by reference mainly to the Judaeo-
Christian tradition within which philosophical discussion on religion has really been developed. Discussing other religious traditions would anyhow be not
essential to a minimal case for including religious
instruction in liberal education. For all we need to
do for this is to prove one religion worthy and we will
have our case even if only in terms of that religion.
However, I am in sympathy with such contemporary
attempts as that by John Hick (see Hick, 1973, 1976)to
show that the major world religions make truth-claims
ultimately of the same transcendent reality, such that
their differences may be regarded as prima facie and
ascribed to cultural accretions and differences in mere
perspective and emphasis; and therefore that particular
doctrines, such as the Incarnation in Christianity,
that seem too particularistic to fit into this unified
cosmic religious view, could warrantedly be reinterpre-
ted to enable them to fit into the universalistic religious tapestry. I shall not argue the details of such
a thesis. Instead, I shall make a couple of sweeping
remarks: this I think is excusable in view of the
rather protracted discussion of Section II below,which,
I shall shortly explain, will suffice at least to tip
our rational preference in favour of the universalism

3

advocated, however different world religions may appear
to be one from the other.

Now, the basic and distinctive truth-claim
which world religions make in common surely concerns a
transcendent or transnatural and transhuman reality,
before which and in terms of which mankind is to stand
and order their lives in awe and reverence. Beyond
this, I think there are good reasons (as I shall presently argue) for insisting that all such religions,
even non-theistic ones, must and can, without being
problematically inconsistent in the case of non-theistic religions, concede the personhood of ultimate
reality or the absolute in a minimal sense. Now this
upholding of a transcendent, at least minimally personal reality is surely of such paramount significance
as to be capable of binding otherwise differing religions together and of overshadowing and reducing to
triviality the doctrinal differences that nevertheless
exist. Against secular humanism, naturalism and the
like, they agree to a reality that lies beyond the
natural realm - already a colossal stride forward,
leave alone the personhood of God they all arguably
also assert. Anyway, beyond the need, I think, to
accede to the minimal sense of a personal deity, what
real differences would doctrinal variations make
(which are necessarily describable only in human language and understandable only in terms of human experience), since they can at most be either merely human
attempts at interpreting and understanding, or what
men can make of divine revelation concerning, a reality
that is in fundamentals utterly beyond human language
and experience to comprehend and describe? How much
nearer the truth can a religion be, even if it were the
best representation of it, beyond the assertion it
shares or should share with other great religions concerning the personal transcendent reality? For in a
sense, all doctrines fall hopelessly short, being merely attempts to say what in essence cannot be said in
human terms.

As regards why I insist that religions assert
a personal deity: it is at least not inconceivable,
with regard to doctrinal differences, that religions
that stress, say, the impersonality of God or ultimate
reality might have the function of complementarily
bringing out the respects in which God's supposed personhood must ultimately be qualified contra the tenden-
cy towards a too anthropomorphic personal conception of
God which does crop up either within a similar, or in

4

other religious traditions. (Hinduism has both the monistic impersonal conception of the Absolute and also the dualistic devotional 'bhakti' approach to a personal God manifested in varieties of incarnations. Even within purported non-theistic religions like Buddhism, Taoism and even Confucianism, there have been near-theistic trends, and the personal conception of God of the Judaeo-Christian tradition has been qualified by philosophical theological treatments that tend towards the impersonal and abstract). If our considerations in Section II indeed necessitate the acceptance of religious universalism, the conceivability of such a reconciliatory move as just exemplified would in itself render it plausible, if we can show it to be the only way out in accounting for doctrinal diversity within the universalistic religious tapestry. Now, the conception of divine personhood must at least imply a centre of awareness, purposiveness and agency; otherwise there can be no sense in the conception as judged by our criterion of 'minimal intelligibility in human terms' stated above (p. 2). For it is not to say anything meaningful to assert divine personhood and yet not mean at least this as regards the deity. This minimal sense of divine personhood therefore would be essential to any conceivable reconciliation of doctrines and religions. For on the minimal intelligibility criterion for sensible assertions, it will be in principle impossible to reconcile theisms with belief in, say, an impersonal Absolute, unless the latter is seen, so I suggest, as an expression - by negation - of a qualifying condition of the personal theistic conception. Why not reconcile by doing away with theism instead, and regarding it as human cultural and anthropomorphic accretions? But while impersonal conceptions of divine reality can be intelligibly seen as a qualifying aspect of divine personhood in the manner suggested, it is absurd or contradictory to conceive of personal conceptions of God being an aspect of impersonal reality. Retaining theism in the proposed religious universalism would therefore be really a reconciliation of religions and doctrines rather than a disruption of some religions, or doctrines within particular religions, in order to universalise some others. It will at any rate be the less wasteful; and surely only justified or really necessary wastes should be tolerated in any attempt to reconcile religions and doctrines.

However, that God must be understood as a person in the minimal sense of being a centre of intentions and awareness and of effective agency will be implied in the manner of testing theistic truth-claims I shall advocate in Part Two (pp. 70-99). If this is right, and assuming theism is reasonably believed in on such tests, then non-theistic religions could and should be regarded in this respect as, say, less perfectly received revelations in the universalistic interpretation of religions (while nonetheless complementing the theistic conception in serving to counterbalance excessive anthropomorphism by their overly stressing divine impersonhood). In some such way, the reconciliation of apparently contradicting or differing doctrines and religions would be conceivable, and therefore should be undertaken.

Now in similar vein, we might consider how the monist idealistic religions, which represent the religious goal as an obliterating of personality to find identity, say with Brahman or the Absolute (whether or not the Absolute is conceived as personal), can be reconciled with those religions with a personal conception of God with their essential implications of an 'I - thou' relationship of worshippers with the diety. I think as far as such monistic religions affect human lives, a sufficient 'dualism' is already present. Thus there is a basic dualism between purported appearance and reality, or between illusion or lower knowledge and truth or higher knowledge; and man's religious quest would, in this life at any rate, still be directed towards the reality that transcends his present lot, with its implied dualism of man and his religious destiny. Even if man is to regard individuality and self as illusory, he (i.e. the self) is still to aspire to true salvation in finding himself identified with the eternal One. Now in view of inter alia the logical contradiction in, and therefore unintelligibility of, the notion of the defining religious emotions of awe and reverence in worship being upheld in a state of complete absorption of the human individual in the Absolute, and also the postulate of the worshipper seeking his own and mankind's ultimate good in his and its utter obliteration: should not and cannot we, in the universalistic reconciling of world religions (and not the abandoning of some religions or doctrines for some others), regard the reference to such obliterating of individuality and personhood as being meant, in ways that necessarily transcend human understanding, to qualify the conception, in overly literal doctrines of theisms, of the individual surviving through eternity glorifying and praising God, etc.; much like what we said of the impersonal conception of God being meant to qualify the necessarily anthropomorphic conception of God as a person? The theistic conception of individuals ultimately surviving through eternity in a state of perfection and harmony with the divine will would at any rate surely be survival of 'personhood' in a radically different sense from that in the human condition. Might it not be that in human language, that could not be otherwise expressed without depicting it as too similar to human personal life, than to assert the utter identification of the self with all other selves in the Absolute?

We must bear in mind in considering all such issues that one is also being overly anthropomorphic in understanding religions if one reads talks of impersonal deity and of the identification of all selves with the Absolute in their literal sense in human language. Just as we should not understand God as a person and heaven, say, as a place perfect in praise and worship in too literal a sense in human language, so we must take similar precaution with interpreting talk of Atman being Brahman, or Nirvana in the human terms of the extinction of self or its identification with the One.

Fundamental too to religions are doctrines concerning the immortality of the soul and the after-life: and regarding these, do religious differences about the nature and mode of the hereafter make enough sense in human terms for them to be significantly divergent? Whatever seem to have been claimed - be it that 'the dead in Christ shall rise' and souls 'return to their bodies' for a 'general resurrection, judgement and consummation' where there will then be 'a new heaven and a new earth', or be it that our destiny will be, through a series of reincarnations determined by our karma, eventually in nirvana or identification with Absolute Being - it is again not inconceivable, and thus the view should be taken if we are compelled on other grounds to accept a religious universalism, that all these are mere attempts to utter humanly inconceivables and inexpressibles in metaphors available in human language. The essence beneath such assertions is conceivably only some such minimal affirmation as that there is a transnatural, eternal destiny for mankind

that is ultimately worthwhile and good, <u>vis-a-vis</u> the
divine being. (John Hick has, on a literal reading of
such assertions, drawn on the resources of major world
religions in order to build up a universal picture of
'death and eternal life' which religions in common may
be affirming; Hick, 1976). There also exist doctrinal
differences of a more practical 'this-worldly' bearing.
Thus what might be interpreted as a denial of the reality of suffering and the natural realm of sense experience in dominant trends in Hinduism would seem plainly contradicted by Christianity which preaches a really
suffering Saviour who was really man and natural,
although also divine. But once we consider such things
as that the denial of the reality of suffering can take
place only where suffering is first experienced and
thereby capable of being denied, and that the point of
the doctrine of self and world denial is precisely to
alleviate suffering among other things, the differences
appear less fundamental and may again be <u>not</u> inconcei-
<u>vably</u> seen as arising from differing emphases only.
Christians too are asked to deny themselves and hate
the world and to set their affections on things above.
And no Hindu would deny that he really lives and experiences this natural life of the senses, illusory
though it nevertheless may be, relative to the true
reality that he believes transcends it.

There is another avenue of consideration - and
this is that which, we said above, could prove definitive for our religious universalism - which religious
universalists like Hick have yet to exploit in advanc-
ing their thesis. This has to do with the repercussion
for religions with universal aspirations - i.e. religions which claim that their particular doctrines and
plans for salvation have exclusive and universal
application for all persons wherever they may be - of
the possible presence of extra-terrestrial biological
persons in the universe. The need for religion to
take seriously the possible existence of such extra-
terrestrial persons (which we will shortly suggest
could even be an internal religious requirement, considering the implications of key doctrines) and the
challenge this would pose for maintaining the intelligibility of the major doctrines of world religions are
themes we shall develop below in the first major section of this part, concerned with alleviating this
possible basic problem of religious intelligibility.
We shall see there that only an universalistic interpretation of religions, that would be compatible with
divine revelation in other modes to such extra-terres-

8

trial communities of persons, would be able to rescue
earthly religions from a doctrinal particularism that
would make nonsense of their central religious truth-
claims, like those regarding a universal creator or
ground of being, or the universal need of natural
persons for salvation. Now once it is conceded that
other religious forms could exist among extra-terrestrial civilisations to point the way to the same transcendent Being for extra-terrestrial persons, even
though they would have to be doctrinally different in
ways not unlike the variations among terrestrial religions, then surely the same should be conceded with
regard to world religions. The various world religious
traditions have also stemmed from civilisations that
originally could have no contact with each other, just
as it would be practically impossible for earth to
have contact with all or most extra-terrestrial communities should these exist (this is the crucial consideration, as we shall see, to our requiring a universalistic interpretation of religions vis-a-vis the existence
of extra-terrestrial persons). (While discussing the
issue concerning extra-terrestrial persons, we will
also deal with an objection which otherwise ought to be
answered here. It is that the universalistic interpretation of religions being advocated might mean rather
the abandoning of religions as we know them, in favour
of an entirely new religion, since the reinterpretation
being envisaged seems a drastic break in identity and
continuity from traditional religions. So, the objection asserts, our universal religion will merely be
just one more religion, adding to the religious plura-
lism (see pp.25-27 below).)

Indications therefore are that we could reject
Hume's contention, in the context of his discussing
the intelligibility of, and the possibility of our
having evidences for, miracles (An Enquiry concerning
Human Understanding, S. X(ii)), that purported proofs
of miracles in the various religious traditions would
if successful cancel each other out, since the proof
of one religion would invalidate other religions, the
different religions being mutually exclusive. The
contrary would be the case by our present indications;
for our view as to the mutual inclusiveness of religions implies that any evidence in favour of the claims
of one religion would mean that much more support for
other religions. Therefore, even though our case, in
this part and the next, for the intelligibility and
initial plausibility of religious truth-claims will be
made by reference only to the Judaeo-Christian tradi-

9

tion, our conclusions will pertain to religion as a universal phenomenon.

We will also be selective in bringing out matters from the Judaeo-Christian tradition for discussion, for I think we can again afford to be selective. With regard to the first criterion of the minimal intelligibility of religious tenets, there is the need, of course, to examine the traditional conceptual problems of Judaeo-Christian theism. But here I think the real obstacle is the problem of evil, which will be discussed in some detail. This has been the main obstacle to religious belief. Indeed many see in it the final disproof of theism (See, for instance, Puccetti, 1964).

Of other traditional conceptual problems, the only ones really crucial to our minimal case for religious intelligibility are those arising from the assertion of transnatural and incorporeal personhood and realm of reality connected with the conceptions of the existence of God and other transnatural beings, and also of the survival of human persons after death. It is clear that sense must be established for these claims before more can be said of other attributes of the transcendent personal God, since if transnatural existence were inconceivable, then whatever other divine attributes that we may conceive would have nothing to qualify and anchor upon. However, once the sense is established, then as long as God can in addition be intelligibly described in enough of some such mutually dependent, implicating and overlapping attributes as his existing 'from everlasting to everlasting', as the creator or ground or sustainer of all being, as almighty (including all-knowing) and all-good (including all-loving), he would be conceivable as a being for man's adoration, utter submission and worship*. Let me

---

* It may be said that in philosophic Hinduism (and therefore _mutatis mutandis_ in Buddhism), the ultimate aim is for man to transcend his personal eternal survival whether it be in the incorporeal state or in multiple physical reincarnations. And divine transcendence is conceived _inter alia_ as the negation of divine personhood and in terms of an abstract and ultimate one true reality into which human individuality also should eventually be absorbed. Even in the Christian tradition, as Rudolf Otto has reminded us (Otto, 1932), Eckhart's concept of God involved such a transcending of the personal. Therefore it may be objected that the notions of a transcendent God and man's eternal religious

elaborate a little on this.

That these attributes overlap and mutually im-
plicate is readily seen. Thus God could not be conceived as all-good if not also seen as the creator and
sustainer of all being. As absolutely dependable ultimate ground and sustainer of all other existents, he
must be all-good and all-powerful. Being almighty and
absolutely dependable sustainer of all, he must be
eternal, without beginning, absolutely independent, and
all-loving. Now, clearly, if God were not almighty and
therefore not the ultimately reliable ground of all
being, without beginning, eternal and absolutely independent, the utter trust and commitment religion
requires of us, including the trust that God will safe-
guard our eternal destiny, would be irrational. Similarly, were he not all-good, his benevolent sustenance
of all could be in doubt, rendering it irrational to
accord him unqualified submission and adoration. And
were he all-good and almighty, but, as per impossible,
not also the source, giver and sustainer of all life
and existence, and the guarantor of our eternal destiny, then we would have no business adoring a God who
minds only his own business, no matter how mighty and
good he is envisaged to be. Such considerations indicate that this family of divine attributes are minimally necessary for religious adherence to be conceivably
sensible and rational, and therefore that all we need,
to render worship of God conceivable and rational, is
a demonstration of sufficient intelligibility for some
such attributes in order to assert, even if only by
implication, more or less the entire family of notions.

---

destiny would not be quite upheld even if we succeed in giving
sense to the conception of transnatural personal existence and
survival.

But my guess is that to talk of transcending even the
state of transnatural personal existence to achieve the impersonal is to verge on contradiction; that is, if the claim that God
and persons have a stake in eternity is to assert anything at all.
The same may be observed in the related claim in the Western traditions that God is timeless. Now if to retain the sense, say of
the sequence of events, necessary for any conception of personal
agency is to be involved in time, then to talk of God's transcending   time is to drop any reference to God's personhood and
relations to his creation. Indeed it is to drop any claim to
divine reality at all at least in-as-far as that reality is
conceived as related to events in the universe (See Pike, 1970).

Now our intended discussion of the problem of evil is meant to render internally coherent this family of divine attributes by suggesting a way to resolve the apparent contradiction between God's purported goodness and love, and his omnipotence (and between the corresponding implications, as noted above, of these attributes) in the face of evil in the universe. In so doing, we will also say enough to resolve the apparent contradiction between the notion of divine omnipotence and that of created moral agents' having freewill (See pp. 53-58). Once these apparently blatant contradictions are shown to be resolvable, there is little more that need be indicated to uphold the intelligibility of the family of divine attributes. For there surely are enough corresponding attributes recognisable in the human situation - and such attributes as the e are precisely those that must have initially given rise to those humanly postulated attributes of God - to be the experiential basis for the leaps of thought and imagination that are necessary if the human mind is ever to somewhat bridge the great gulf of understanding between the natural and the transnatural, in the quest to develop on revelatory promptings and to understand somewhat revelatory events, assuming God exists and reveals himself to man. Thus, we surely know in our experience what it is like to wield power and to submit to the very powerful, knowledgeable and capable. We also experience what it is like to be somewhat good and loving, and to benefit from the goodness and love of others. Now, for God to be all-good and almighty is for him to possess like attributes, even though to an infinite degree expectedly beyond our natural experience and cognisance. The latter lapse of understanding need not worry us unduly since we do understand the sort of thing it is that we do not understand. The fact that there are within the human situation those persons whose power, understanding and goodness far exceed the average so as to be already wonder-inspiring should suffice as an experiential basis for analogically conceiving God's infinite and wonderful possession of like

---

In any case, in the reconciliation of religions we suggested earlier, talk of God's transcendence of both personhood and time could, and therefore should, be regarded as significant only in qualifying a too anthropomorphic understanding of the existence of a personal God and other persons in the eternal state.

attributes. Similarly, we surely experience what it is
for something to be the foundation of other things, or
for someone to create, say, some original work of art.
Conceiving God as the creator and sustainer of all is
therefore to imagine analogically, with due allowance
made for what in the matter is after all expectedly
and understandably beyond our ken, God as ultimately
that 'in whom we live and move and have our being'.
And as regards his existing independently and eternally
without a beginning, I have deliberately evaded the
possible conceptual difficulties of using the term
'necessary existence'. For pace J.N. Findlay (Findlay,
1955),I think it is not necessary for theists to conceive God's existence as literally 'necessary', in the
logician's sense applicable only to propositions and
not existent beings and things, in order to bring out,
in human and therefore understandably inadequate terms
some minimally sufficient sense of God's existing independently 'from everlasting to everlasting'. Indeed,
the very fact that 'necessary' is attributable only to
propositions should rather lead us to conclude that the
term cannot have been applied to describe God in that
sense, since God is conceived as existent reality.
(Findlay's critique - that since 'necessary' can only
be attributed to propositions, God cannot exist, for
necessity is one of his defining attributes - therefore
fails. I hear however that Findlay has since abandoned
the position.) Now, in our experience, we know what it
is for contingent beings to be dependent and to have
beginnings and ends, with the accompanying insecurities
and fears, untimeliness and transciencies. We also
know by some contrast what it is to have relative per-
manence, lastingness and independence, with the consequence of having greater trust and confidence. Now
would not this experiential basis suffice for us to
envisage an extension of this contrast to the limits of
the humanly conceivable, beyond which to leave room -
an understandable and intelligible strategy - for awe,
mystery and faith as regards an 'infinite' extension
of the same in God? Hard to understand as it may be to
us - for in the natural realm, it is true that all
existents thrive under severely contrasting limitations
- we are confronted, in surely intelligible claims to
divine revelation or religious intuition, with the conception of God's 'independent' and 'eternal' existence,
which we partially understand by the analogy of the
temporary and dependent as contrasted with the relatively permanent and independent in human experience.
Who is to rule out the conceivability of such a being
existing in the transnatural order merely on the ground

13

that in the natural realm the only similar notion of logical necessity is an attribute only of propositions? Isn't it conceivable that in this matter there may be some ultimate divine facts (which we somewhat understand on the partial experiential basis described) which we must ultimately just accept, having confronted some such being, say through religious intuition, revelation or experience? And it could be _inter alia_ precisely because in the natural experience nothing that exist can exist necessarily in the logician's sense applicable to propositions that the awesome idea of one who exists 'necessarily', though only so analogically, in a somewhat similar and yet essentially different, ultimately inexplicable sense, can inspire us to worship; for by this also would the one be transcendent, and ultimately tremendous and mysterious.

Now that the family divine attributes discussed above are intelligible and assertable, do we really need to say and understand more of God before we are rightly overwhelmed in wonder and awe, provided we make sense and are convinced of his existence as transnatural and incorporeal person? In any case, how much more other than these attributes can be said of him in human terms apart from the sense human language may imperfectly provide concerning his transnatural personal existence and the possibility of man's partaking in such an existence in his eternal destiny? Of course religions should and do attempt to say and, indeed where revelatory hints and promptings insist, they should try to stretch human language and analogies to their sensible limits in such understanding while being wary of going beyond those limits, and recognising when religious over-enthusiasm in this regard has in fact produced excesses resulting in utterances verging on nonsense and the ridiculous that have marred essentially meaningful religions.

Concerning the issue of transnatural and incorporeal existence and man's survival of bodily death, there have already been much favourable and adequately suggestive discussions in contemporary philosophical theology (See for instances Lewis, 1973; Price, 1971, chap. 5, 6.) Therefore rather than review old arguments, I shall be brief and offer a novel case for the intelligibility of the conceptions.

But before discussing the traditional problems in Section III below, I want in Section II to examine, as mentioned, the problems of doctrinal intelligibility

14

that the presence of extra-terrestrial biological persons would pose. I shall do this in a rejoinder to
Roland Puccetti, who in chapter five of his book
Persons (Puccetti, 1968) has scored a first in tracing
in detail certain major conceptual problems for traditional religions, given the plausibility of the belief
in extra-terrestrial persons he himself in earlier
chapters of the book had established. Now, even if it
be said that it is still too speculative to base the
belief in extra-terrestrial persons, as Puccetti mainly
does, on the fact there are 'one hundred million sites
of (possible) extra-terrestrial intelligence in our
galaxy alone' (Op. Cit. p. 128), there would be internal religious considerations which could render it
a matter of conceptual or doctrinal consistency to
believe such intelligences exist. For wouldn't it be
inconsistent and conceptually strained to envisage an
almighty, all wise and good God, whose creative purposiveness, orderliness and fruitfulness are claimed to
be evident all around us on this our planet, bringing
into being the vast universe the extent of which we
cannot as yet imagine, wherein exist at least one
hundred million sites of possible extra-terrestrial
persons in our galaxy plus the millions upon millions
of such sites in all the other galaxies known and unknown, but being content only to people the planet
earth? Wouldn't such a cosmic anomaly, waste and void
be additional data to aggravate, say, the problem of
evil, since they suggest randomness or a lack of purposiveness in cosmic development, or a lack of the
creative potency or moral goodness to actualise many
more of such religiously acknowledged intrinsic goods
as the members of the human race? (Religion has of
course asserted the existence of 'spiritual' persons,
e.g. angels, but we are here concerned with the envisaged cosmic void within the natural physical universe).

Anyhow, if doctrinal intelligibility can be
defended contra Puccetti's criticisms, it would be
worthwhile doing so even if only to eliminate a possible futuristic direction of fresh doubts in our attempt
to secure a case for the respectability of religious
truth-claims. After all, that extra-terrestrial persons exist is itself a respectable scientific expectation which will never in fact be falsified, since however much we will know about conditions in outer space,
there will always remain the possibility of non-human
biological persons existing elsewhere in the infinite
regions we will not as yet know. There will always
remain the scientifically respectable anticipation that

all the reasons we could have for religion might be
nullified by the discovery of extra-terrestrial civilisations. Therefore, if this nagging doubt can be
eliminated by our theoretical reconciling of religious
'truths' to that eventuality, the exercise will be
worthwhile even if it were a mere academic affair.
Also the sort of problems Puccetti has said religions
will face as a consequence of it has yet to be taken
seriously by religious apologists. And the discovery
of extra-terrestrial civilisations would be phenomenal
for religions in that even if they would still be intelligible in that light, drastic revisions in our conceptions of them, as already indicated, would be necessary. Therefore, our characterisation of the significance of religious truth-claims and religious education
can hardly afford to ignore this possible discovery.
Besides, we said that the discussion will constitute
our crucial support for Hick's sort of religious universalism. The universalism will of course have important bearings on the question what and how to teach,
once religious instruction is shown to have liberal
educational import.

We have so far outlined our program for the
rest of Part One. In Part Two, we shall continue our
apology for religion and suggest a way by which religion can meet our second criterion for the admissibility of religious instruction in the liberal curriculum,
i.e. the criterion of the initial evidential plausibility of religious truth-claims (Cf. p.3). As
will be indicated, our case for the intelligibility of
religious assertions will significantly depend on the
success of our arguments in Part Two.

II   A FUTURISTIC CONCEPTUAL PROBLEM: EXTRA-TERRES-
     TRIAL PERSONS AND DOCTRINAL INTELLIGIBILITY

Puccetti argues that the belief in extra-
terrestrial persons, combined with the correct analysis
of the concept of persons, would undermine religious
beliefs in a manner that threatens an entire jettison-
ing of religions (Op. Cit. p. 144). A religion is an
entire tradition from its founder up to the present.
It forms a living terrestrial tradition the development
of which has necessarily to be particularistic. Abandoning all particularistic beliefs would therefore be
tantamount to abandoning religion itself. Also, particularism is necessary if the religion is to be instrumental in our lives. But with the bright prospects of

non-human biological communities existing elsewhere in the universe, a religion with universal aspirations has also to extend its scope of reference to members of such communities, who, according to Puccetti's earlier analysis in the book, should qualify as 'persons', and thus should be considered as religiously important as humans. It is Puccetti's opinion that the necessary particularism of religions makes it impossible for them to be really universal in this sense. For if a religion is really nothing more than a terrestrial system of beliefs having only terrestrial reference then, he maintains, the God-concept loses all its force, since God can no more be regarded as the supreme master of the universe. Also, particularism implies exclusiveness, so that indications are that religions by their nature positively suggest this.

Puccetti discusses the particularism of religions at length. There is first the observation that nothing in the revelation of purportedly universal religions indicates the existence of persons other than humans in the universe - at any rate, nothing that is beyond dispute and accepted by believers. Though silence on the matter does not amount to a logical disproof of religions, it generates 'a profound suspicion that these terrestrial faiths are no more than that' (p. 126). The discussion then points to the practical impossibility of earthlings ever reaching extra-terrestrial communities with the preaching of a religion, so that if an earthly religion is ever to aspire to universality, then either an identical tradition has to, or enough key features of the tradition have to, recur among such communities. Now, the former is a conceptual impossibility, while the latter Puccetti shows to be absurd by reference to the particularism of the tenets of major religions (e.g. doctrines like the Incarnation and the Crucifixion in Christianity) analysed in terms of the person-concept.

Two sorts of theistic answer to Puccetti's onslaught have been mooted in two reviews of the book. One suggests that religious doctrines, without any reinterpretation of them, could be argued to be compatible with the discovery of extra-terrestrial persons. Thus Alasdiar MacIntyre (MacIntyre, 1968) asserts that the beings on other planets, if there are such, may well have been informed of the Incarnation directly by God, if there is one'. 'Or else . . . they may all be unfallen and in their paradisal innocence not need to know of the Incarnation'. It is unlikely that this

17

sort of defence will work. Puccetti has said enough to suggest that MacIntyre's alternatives would likewise meet with insuperable difficulties. How could the Incarnation be understood unless placed in the context of the religious tradition? Even if it could, would the doctrine, separated from the Christian tradition, be Christianity? And how could we make sense of the notion of God communicating an entire terrestrially 'lived-out' tradition to extra-terrestrials? If, however, the Incarnation were not necessary among extra-terrestrial civilisations, then whatever religious systems might exist, they would not be orthodox Christianity since the latter regards it as the unique manifestation of God's image. These considerations suggest that Christianity in the original form cannot be made compatible with the discovery of extra-terrestrial persons.

The other sort of defence is more promising. It says that fundamentalism can be and has been dispensed with when interpreting religious doctrines (though not to the extent of resorting to the radical reductionistic reinterpretation of religions we rejected (pp. x-xi)), and that religions faced with the prospects of extra-terrestrials existing might go around the difficulties by means of some such reinterpretation. Thus, Richard Wallace, in his review of Puccetti's book (Wallace, 1969) accuses him of ignoring 'the fact that some theologians would claim that a "fundamentalist" approach to doctrinal formulation is unjustifiable and theologically inept'. Wallace then suggests a possible reinterpretation of the Incarnation which makes it 'unique (only) within the history of our planetary system', so that beings in other planetary systems might be given other manifestations of God's image. An objection to this would be that such reinterpretations would not be strictly Christianity as the recognised tradition defines it, so that it would not be Christianity that is being defended once they are accepted. And even allowing this as a defence, this line of thinking would finally reduce Christianity to unrecognisable insignificance so that the end result could be the disappearance of Christianity from within. This is a pertinent objection and must be surmounted if Wallace's sort of defence is to work.

My aim is to trace a possible theistic line of defence against Puccetti's criticisms which will crucially depend on the strengthening of the sort of defence suggested by Wallace. I shall first discuss the implications of the silence of religions about the presence of extra-terrestrial persons. I shall then discuss the purported need for the replication of features and identity among extra-terrestrial communities for a religion to have universal aspirations.

Now, does it follow that the absence of reference to non-human persons, if such exist, within religious traditions is sufficient to make us profoundly suspicious that terrestrial religions are no more than that? But non-reference does not amount to a denial, so that, as Puccetti admits, the silence of religious traditions on the matter does not amount to a logical disproof of religious claims. If this is the case, the situation, as it is, is indicatively neutral, unless good reasons are given to show why the silence does generate suspicion. Puccetti's main reason may be detected in the question, 'Why have the adherents to these faiths been allowed to think down through the ages that a drama involving only God and homo sapiens was being played out on the cosmic stage?' (p. 125). Implied is the further claim that, granted that extra-terrestrial persons should be regarded as religiously significant, it is imperative for religious traditions to contain a revelation regarding such persons. This is seen in Puccetti's assertion that 'the only way around (his) criticism, it seems, is to deny that the existence of extra-terrestrials really have religious significance' (Ibid). The implication is, therefore, that once the existence of such beings has religious significance, this should have been highlighted within a religious tradition.

Now, it is simply a matter of interpretation on Puccetti's part to claim that adherents of religious faiths have been allowed to think the drama on the cosmic stage has been played only between homo sapiens and God. The fact surely is simply that no reference has been made to extra-terrestrials. (And I have suggested above that given the knowledge of the expanse of the cosmos and the multiplicity of possible locations of biological persons within it, it might be the case that religious doctrines imply that humans are not the only natural persons. But I don't have to press this point). Now, silence on a matter can be regarded as a denial of it only in situations where an advantage is unfairly gained by a deliberate suppression of information, like a wife not telling her husband about her affair with another man. It can be taken as a neglect on the informer's part only where the information is really essential knowledge. But in our case, it will be shown that knowledge of extra-terrestrials is not really necessary for religious practice. Regarding the second reason, it is highly disputable that if extra-terrestrial persons should be accepted as religiously significant, there should be a revelation concerning them. This would be the case indeed if terrestrial beings were meant also to be the preachers of   salvation to extra-terrestrials. But this is hardly implied by the admission that extra-terrestrials are as religiously important as humans. Puccetti has himself quoted facts and figures to show the practical impossibility of earthlings ever reaching extra-terrestrials with a message. 'It would require almost one hundred thousand years for a radio wave to reach the furthest star in our own galaxy, and about two million years to reach the nearest other galaxy' (p. 136). Extra-terrestrials could be regarded as religiously significant in the sense of an admission that the <u>same</u> God can be left to deal with extra-terrestrials independently of us and 'save' them if need be in whatever manner he thinks fit. (I don't think it at all necessary, if a religion is to have universal aspirations, for it to have identical traditions or replicative features among extra-terrestrial communities, or failing both to stand in need of the possibility of preaching the earthly tradition among such communities. This will be argued later.)

Positive reasons could, at any rate, be given by the theist as to why there has been no mention of extra-terrestrial persons in religious revelations. Puccetti rejects Ninian Smart's thesis that the 'essential historicity' of Christianity 'precludes the revelation of factual matters beyond the scientific understanding of men in ancient Palestine'. (Smart, 1961). As regards the revelation of facts concerning the existence of extra-terrestrials, Puccetti argues that men of the ancient Near East did have sufficient understanding of biochemistry and astrophysics to grasp the meaning of such a revelation. Such knowledge, at any rate, need not be gained scientifically, so that God could have spoken about the matter in the same way as he has been claimed to have spoken about other matters.

But the essential historicity of Christianity could be seen, on other grounds, to preclude the possibility of revelation about extra-terrestrials. These hinge on the admissibility of certain less orthodox interpretations of the doctrine regarding the mode of

divine revelation and here, as will be recognised,
Wallace's sort of defence becomes apposite. Puccetti's
case rests on the orthodox 'propositional' view of revelation, according to which God reveals truth-proposi-
tions in a manner not unlike the business executive
dictating sentences to his stenographer. Thus he is
able to argue that since men at that time, generally
considered, could have understood the revelation regarding extra-terrestrial persons, Smart's sort of
defence won't do. But to describe the view of divine
revelation as orthodox is really to contrast it with
more modern, less established views, which might make
Smart's sort of defence appropriate. It has however
to be argued that such non-orthodox views can be
regarded as part of and not unidentifiably discontinuous with the Christian tradition.

Now, the boundary between orthodoxy and non-
orthodoxy is never stable nor clear, as Puccetti has
himself pointed out (p. 140). What is non-orthodoxy
today might become orthodoxy tomorrow, and perhaps vice
versa. And if, as Puccetti rightly maintains, a religious tradition 'is not only what the founder taught or
the original canonical documents say' but is 'everything that it has become up to the present' (p. 131)
(and, we may add, what it will become in the future),
then the question of the admissibility of more novel
interpretations of doctrines as being within religious
traditions must always be regarded as open. Jesus,
after all, wrote nothing and what has been purported
to be his own claims about his status is not beyond
interpretative dispute. The original interpretation of
doctrines were formulated after his life-time by the
first Christians, so that they could be regarded as
rudimentary. Later developments in doctrinal interpretation by abler men should then be always regarded as
more adequate. And if one is to attack a belief, it is
the best possible representation of it that one must
consider.

There must indeed be a limit to changes in doctrinal reinterpretation. If we are to avoid ascribing
inconsistency to Puccetti, we have to take it that,
though he has not explicitly stated this, he has implied in his discussion that while a religion might
change and develop, certain key-defining doctrines must
not in the process be too watered down, if it is to
maintain its identity. This is suggested by the importance with which he regards the difficulties a religion would encounter, faced with the prospects of

extra-terrestrials existing, if it is to substantially retain key doctrines like the Incarnation. What is left to be done, however, is to indicate the limits within which reinterpretation of doctrines is permissible.

There has to be a substantive residue of meaning left of original doctrines if whatever new interpretations are to be recognisably Christian. In other words, there has to be a core residue of doctrinal orthodoxy. For instance, Jesus Christ has always featured in the tradition as in some sense uniquely related to God according to some sensible interpretation of the 'Father-Son' concept. Christians have always seen Christ as centrally featured both in the Old and New Testaments, the former pointing forward to and the latter looking backward at the Messiah. There can be no Christianity without Christ understood as having a special relationship with the transcendent personal God. This is why it is at once dubious whether Christian atheists or certain 'death-of-God' theologians or those 'Christians' advocating the reductionistic secularist views of religion we mentioned (Cf. pp.x-xi) are really Christians. But believers' understanding and interpretation of the exact mode of this relationship have and can be changed. However watered down the end result of such changes is, it should remain recognisable as a sensible, perhaps improved review of original doctrines surrounding the person of Jesus in his relationship with the transcendent personal God. As regards the doctrine regarding divine revelation, the residue to be retained is surely only that God has and does communicate with men. Thus, if a new interpretation emerges that says God does not communicate with men and that what has been regarded as revelation were due to men's own imagination, then it would not be a Christian doctrine. But if it says that God had made use of men's imagination to communicate to them, then it would have retained the required residue of meaning.

The objection that such flexibility in interpretation of doctrines will immunise Christianity from quite a lot of rational criticism and might therefore render it disreputable cannot be applied to the present discussion. For here, we are tracing the effects of the existence of extra-terrestrial persons on religious thinking, and the allowance for doctrinal reinterpretation happens to be characteristic of this thinking. It might be that the mode of thinking will render the entire religious system unfalsifiable, but we have said

22

that the religious tradition does place limits to such reinterpretation, so that in as much as it does, it is open to falsification.

The way is now open for us to examine Puccetti's onslaught vis-a-vis a fairly recent sort of reinterpretation regarding the doctrine of revelation. John Hick has labelled it 'the non-propositional view' - one that has become widespread, as Hick points out, within Protestant Christianity in the present century, and which claims its sources in the thought of the 16th century reformers. (Hick, 1963, pp. 70-77). On the non-propositional view, revelation is seen as God entering the sphere of human experience and acting in human history. Theological propositions, like 'Jesus is God the Son', are not God-dictated but are only human attempts at formulating a meaning to revelatory events. The view is not that Christianity can be entirely 'non-propositional', but that theological propositions contain only the meaning men have tried to give to revelatory facts. (This is not to say that theological meanings must therefore be thoroughly or mostly given in terms of men's experience. If those 'revelatory facts' are authentically God-arranged, then their purpose would be to point beyond to their transcendent source; so that although the bases for human interpretation of them must necessarily be in human experience, they serve merely to inspire the receptive and imaginative mind to the contemplation and attempted utterance of things unutterable in fundamental ways. This view of revelation therefore is not incompatible with our earlier insistence that in pressing the criterion of doctrinal sensibility, allowance must be made for a high degree of unintelligibility when judging doctrines, quite inescapably, in human terms.)

Now, on some such view of revelation, it is clear that the fact that humanity, generally considered, could have understood the existence of extra-terrestrial persons, is no longer sufficient to rebut Smart's sort of defence. For, the theist can maintain, the members of a particular race, or more accurately, the chosen few of that race might not have themselves the capacity for the sort of understanding necessary to being instrumental in such a revelation, whatever else other persons or members of other races were capable of. Nor can it be said that an almighty God could have temporarily over-ridden this difficulty, for we have already indicated above that revelation regarding extra-terrestrial persons, assuming that such exist, is

not all that important to religions. At any rate, there
surely was no real point in Biblical days for God to
have revealed anything about extra-terrestrials. Notions like space travel were inconceivable, and even
in modern times Puccetti has pointed out the practical
impossibility of earthlings ever reaching extra-terrestrials with a message.

Puccetti, however, cannot maintain that a religion is a living tradition up to everything it is at
present and at the same time treat the religious dogmas
and tenets within the tradition as final and complete.
The tradition will continue to grow, and the possibility of the existence of non-human biological persons
being accepted and incorporated within the tradition
will always remain a possibility. There is nothing in
the books to insist that revelation must always precede
scientific discovery. It is pertinent only to say that
revelation would then lack point. But this merely
shows that revelation would be unnecessary.

To this Puccetti might object that the kind of
conceptual expansion involved in, say, the Christian
religion's recognition of the existence of such communities would result in nothing recognisably Christian
surviving. Answering this objection involves considering the next part of Puccetti's analysis.

Assuming that extra-terrestrial communities do
exist, is it really necessary, for a religion which
regards them as religiously significant, to have replicas of features or identity among such communities,
once communication of the terrestrial tradition to
extra-terrestrials is practically impossible? If the
answer is affirmative, then Puccetti's examination of
the possibility of having such replicas, especially
with regard to the defining doctrines of Christianity,
like the Incarnation (pp. 136-143), has successfully
demonstrated the whole matter to be ludicrous, in the
face of the essential particularism of religious traditions.

We must note at once that Puccetti would agree
that it is enough for a religion, which accepts the
significance of extra-terrestrial persons, to recognise
that such persons are 'also capable of salvation in
God's eyes', have 'the same creaturely relation to Him
as men have' and do 'stand in a moral relationship to
God, just as men do'. (p. 125). What he wants further
to assert is that this entails that the terrestrial

24

religion's 'scheme of salvation' must have universal application in a similar form.

Now, the theist might deny the necessity for such replication of features and traits among extra-terrestrial communities for a religion to agree that non-human persons deserve salvation, just like humans. A distinction has here to be made between, (1) an earthly religion regarding extra-terrestrials as in God's eyes equally important as human beings, and (2) an earthly religious tradition claiming universal application in the same mode and form. Now, contrary to what Puccetti seems to think, the former position does not entail the latter.

While the understanding and mode of worship within a religious tradition is necessarily particularistic, the object of worship, God, the creator of all, is universal, in the sense that he exists for all persons in the universe to seek and understand. And, granted that extra-terrestrials are just as important in God's eyes, and that they should be regarded as within the scope of salvation of such a God, it hardly follows that the <u>actual</u> <u>scheme</u> of salvation must be identical or similar to that of the earthly tradition. In fact, it might even be reasonably argued that implicit in the admittance of the partiality, at the various stages, of men's understanding of God, and the view that revelation is more or less limited to what particular men in historical contexts could understand or imagine, is the denial that the terrestrial scheme need have replicas among extra-terrestrial communities. For if what men have understood or imagined of God and how God has dealt with men had necessarily been determined by the historicity of the situation, then it should not be surprising if God had not dealt with extra-terrestrial civilisations in an identical or even closely similar fashion. It follows that if God had not intended earthlings to preach the terrestrial scheme of salvation to extra-terrestrials (which can be assumed since the communication of the earthly religion has been shown to be practically impossible), then he need not be expected to intend similar schemes for salvation among non-human communities. The way is open for Wallace's sort of doctrinal reinterpretation.

But as the religious tradition enlarges to take account in some such way of the existence of extra-terrestrials, would not what finally emerges be completely unidentifiable as Christianity? If, say, it be

finally accepted that (1) Christianity is only one
scheme for salvation applicable only to terrestrials
(and perhaps just one of many other schemes among
terrestrials themselves, as we suggested earlier on);
and (2) that other more or less different religions,
revolving perhaps around extra-terrestrial personalities who are counterparts to Jesus Christ, exist for
the salvation of extra-terrestrials; would not what
finally emerges reduce Christianity to unrecognisable
insignificance in the face of the countless numbers of
extra-terrestrial communities there may be? What would
happen to, say, doctrines like Christ being the king of
kings and lord of lords, the alpha and omega, the
eternal judge, the being without whom there was nothing
made that was made?

Now, in view of our earlier discussion regarding the limits within which doctrinal reinterpretation
is legitimate, we may say in defence that: firstly,
such a conceptual expansion is made possible by a
legitimately Christian 'non-propositional' concept of
divine revelation; and, secondly, the expansion of
ideas does not involve the abandoning of the required
residue in meaning and orthodoxy of the doctrines
regarding Jesus. While the Incarnation as representing
some sense in which God has manifested himself to men is
the required residue to be retained, some doctrines
that have grown around this concept, like that of Jesus
being the king of kings, seem merely to represent the
adoration with which believers have regarded him. They
are expressed with poetic overtones and feature more in
hymns than in plain statements of theological truths.
Concepts like Jesus being the eternal judge or the
author of everything there is could continue to feature
in some such way. Since he is, in some sense, the God-
man, then in the sense that he represents God, he is
the eternal Creator and Judge.

True, the kind of Christianity that will emerge
might involve a change that is unprecedented. But
excessive novelty by itself would not, at any rate, en-
danger the maintenance of an identity. A distinction
must be made between (1) the situation where an old
concept is forgotten and an exceedingly novel one moved
into its place, and (2) the situation which would arise
where a tradition develops and changes, but all the
while maintaining a historical continuity, until it
finally emerges with very novel reinterpretations of
the key doctrines, while nevertheless retaining a
residue of orthodoxy and meaning. In the latter case,

it would be possible to trace the historical development of believers' understanding of doctrines, and it
would be a recognisably Christian tradition that is
being traced. Just as within Judaism the concept of a
tribal God, by continuous stages, has developed into
that of an universal God (unrecognisable, if you like,
to the previous one), so doctrines centering on the
person of Jesus could undergo some such changes. Just
as we can regard Christianity, as we now know it, as
being the result of a section of Judaism having expand-
ed till it includes the gentiles within its scope of
reference, so we could conceivably imagine it incorporated within a universal system embracing all extra-
terrestrial (and terrestrial) faiths. Whatever it
would become, it would still be a recognisably 'expand-
ed' Christianity as long as, say, the Incarnation were
still regarded as 'God became man' in some sense. In
other words, our solution to the problem is in refit-
ting earthly religions into a common cosmic religious
tapestry that would of course require the universalistic interpretation of world religions advocated in the
preceding section.

III   TRADITIONAL CONCEPTUAL PROBLEMS

       Having secured the intelligibility of religion
against the threatening repercussions of a scientifically respectable anticipated finding, we may now re-
vert with more assurance to our discussion of traditional religious conceptual problems. In sub-section
one below, I shall discuss the conceptual problems
concerning the notion of transnatural and incorporeal
personhood, and then, in sub-section two, the problem
of evil will be extendedly examined.

(i)   Transnatural Personhood and States, and the
       Notion of Death being Survived

       Problems arise from the conception of incorpo-
real personhood and realm of reality inherent in the
notion of a transcendent God and order of reality. If
sense can be given to the conception, I think we will
already be at an adequate though minimal understanding
of transcendent and transnatural personhood and state.
For keeping in mind what we said before (Cf.p.11 foot-note)
concerning the unintelligibility of the idea of God's
and other persons' 'transcending' personality altogether, surely the transnatural element in the notion of

27

divine transcendence cannot be too dissimilar to the sense of incorporeal personal existence and states, if we can establish it. Surely, whatever more the notion of divine transcendence might imply must somehow be only so much more of such transcendings of the natural conditions of personhood and states. Anyhow, what more can and need be said from the human perspective beyond the conceiving of this minimal transcending as a sufficent experiential basis for accepting the humanly inexplicable conception of divine transcendence?

Now semantic attacks have more been levelled at the conception of incorporeal personhood, although the claim to a transnatural and immaterial realm of reality, that presumably satisfies the environmental conditions for interpersonal interaction and personal existence of 'heavenly beings', seems equally problematic. Ordinary language strictures have been applied here, such as that our concept of persons presupposes the necessity of corporeal criteria and conditions for personal identity and continuity, inter-personal interaction and agency. God is however conceived as incorporeal and yet a person who interacts with humans and who exerts effective agency within the natural order. The argument for the necessity of bodily contiguity for personal identity through time is usually given in attempts to discredit the conception of man's survival of bodily death, itself a central religious tenet (which we will discuss in the same context); this contention can also be used to attack the concept of divine personhood since it further illustrates how our ordinary concept of persons might be inextricably tied in with corporeality.

Such objections can for our purpose be answered here in a general and summary way via giving some initial supportive indications. Beyond this, our definitive answer, as will be explained, will arise in conjunction with the main thrust of Part Two. Now, if we remember that it is the intelligibility of theistic truth-claims and not their demonstrability that now concerns us, we should realise that once incorporeal personhood and states of being are shown to be conceivable, we would have a case even where it has to be conceded that such incorporeal states are in principle undemonstrable within the human experience. Assuming that theism were thoroughly a human invention, it would be pertinent to say that if such transnatural existences are in principle undemonstrable, humans could have no basis for postulating them, and as such their conceivability would be a moot point. But we have said that revelation is a central theistic tenet. Now I want to suggest that the very facts of our existence as persons, and of the existence of the cosmos within the natural order, would in themselves suffice as a minimal experiential basis to render conceivable the postulate of incorporeal, transnatural persons and states of being. This is so despite that the same material conditions for personhood necessary in the natural realm would of course be unobtainable in the postulated transnatural realm. If the natural realm of rational centres of consciousness and things exists, where in the case of humans, memory and corporeal contiguity form the basis for personal identity, and all this is of course conceivable; then surely we can on that broad experiential basis alone conceive of other states of existence where, say, beings somewhat analogous to persons in our sense maintain their contiguity and identity in terms of memory and also other non-natural and incorporeal media analogous to physical bodies and environments.* If the fact of our personhood and inter-personal interaction is an existential given we must just ultimately accept, could it not be that there may be other similar given conditions, such as other dimensions of reality where analogous media for personhood and interpersonal interaction exist? If in merely finding ourselves in the existential given we have to accede to its possibility and facticity, however perplexing the situation ultimately may (and does) seem to us, how could we exclude the possibility

---

* It may be said that conceiving God as having a kind of body and being in need of a kind of environment for personal contiguity and agency, even if these are non-natural and 'spiritual' media, would hardly tally with the divine attributes of, say, omnipotence, omnipresence and omniscience. For corporeality of any sort implies limitations in these and other respects. But isn't saying this to presuppose a too anthropomorphic understanding of the analogy with the natural conditions of personhood? Beyond the mere conceivability of the analogical postulate, we have necessarily to remain agnostic and assent to doctrines about the all-pervasiveness or immanence of the divine person, as long as these are not necessarily negated by the postulate. For instance, God's 'spiritual' media of personhood could well be coterminous with the extent of his omnipresence and pervasiveness.

that we may likewise have to accept as given the existence of a transcendent realm of things where the divine person and other possible beings exist satisfying
whatever conditions of personhood there must be?
Doesn't one realised possibility at least render it
possible and conceivable that there may exist another
analogous possibility, even if it does not as yet
warrant it as a rationally compelling hypothesis to be
seriously entertained? As a human discovery, the
postulate, it is true, might be in fact practically,
if not logically, impossible; since the transcendent is
by definition beyond human experience and it would be
hard to envisage legitimate, totally natural experiential grounds for perceiving, however imperfectly, the
transcendent. But it has to be conceded at least that
the postulate is not inconceivable pending grounds for
belief in divine revelation.

An objection may be that such postulates of
transnatural 'bodies' and 'environments' amount to
double-talk, since the model is still inextricably
corporeal and cannot have sense away from the physico-
temporal context. Now we readily concede this if it
merely means that we have to talk of those purported
truths in terms of analogies available in our natural
experience. But if it means to disallow even the mere
conceivability and possibility that the analogies could
have an application in a wider totality of different
orders of 'things', and to rule out at the start talk,
say, of 'spiritual media or substance', then I think it
has arbitrarily stipulated a definition of the transnatural to mean the absence of any conceivable content
or state other than the natural. For religions do
talk, claiming divine revelation for it, of the transnatural realm or state of being, the conceivability of
which, we argued above, cannot be ruled out given our
natural experience. Our appeal to analogy may also
give rise to the usual objection that an analogy can be
drawn only when both the items being compared are sufficiently known in order for something as yet unknown in
one to be postulated on the basis of what is in fact
the case in the more fully known other item. In the
case of the transnatural, the objection is that nothing
of this is known independently of the purported analogy
with the natural order of things. But isn't this again
to conveniently ignore the special circumstances of
religion where divine revelation and divine knowledge
are centrally presupposed? The religious use of analogies presumes, surely, that divine revelation inter
alia contains the assurance that the analogy has point

and application, since what is revealed is done necessarily in analogical language. And God would of course know the other item that is being compared. Thus if it is not inconceivable that revelation concerning a divine person could be true, then the postulate of transnatural persons having, like human persons, analogical 'spiritual bodies and media' for personal contiguity and identity and inter-personal interaction must likewise be not inconceivable.

We should add that our above considerations would have independent and definitive support should the manner of testing religious truth-claims we shall advocate in Part Two be successfully used. For, as will shortly be explained, the successful testing would be coterminous with the demonstrating of _personal_ 'visitations' in the affairs of men from a non-natural existential realm. In such an eventuality, the experiential basis the context of the testing would constitute would provide intelligibility for postulating that whatever necessary conditions there may be for transcendent personhood must in fact be satisfied, whether or not this can be conceived in human terms.

Now our above conclusions would also serve to alleviate the conceptual problems in the claim of men's survival of bodily death. For if sense can be given to the postulate of a transcendent state of personal existence, say with 'spiritual' media for personhood analogous to physical bodies and environments, then it should be conceivable that at death the earthly centre of personal awareness that is the pre-mortem man continues in a 'spiritual' replica of the pre-mortem body that is identical with it in crucial ways, say in memory tract and other essential character attributes. How more exactly this can be is expectedly beyond human comprehension; but God could surely see to it that personal continuity on earth, where the corporeal contiguity that enables it is by no means a matter of the _same_ _material_ persisting, is translated at a crucial moment in death to continue in a different order and medium that nevertheless is guaranteed by him to enable the identification of the post-mortem individual with the pre-mortem one. And because it would be this particular person whom God would presumably be attending to and determining his personal translation - even his very hairs would be numbered -, there would be no question of identification problems arising in the after-life in a situation where more than one post-

mortem 'spiritual' replica-persons of the pre-mortem
one are actualised and where the usual bodily contiguity would not be available to settle the issue. If such
multiple replicas did actualise, then it presumably
could only mean that the physical impossibility of the
previous actualising on earth of two or more persons
with identical histories had been the case. God would
not play games and cause confusion by creating multiple
instant Tans in 'heaven'. (This observation, inciden-
tally, would apply also to similar identification
'problems' arising in the postulate of multiple identical resurrections; see Clarke, 1971; and Hick, 1972).

And would it involve too much a stretching of
ordinary language to conceive a transcendent God's
effective agency in the natural realm? But even within
our natural experience there are phenomena, like tele-
kinesis, which conceivably could give a sense to the
postulate of an analogous transcendent, incorporeal
person producing effects within the natural and physical order. Anyhow there is the general point that on
mind-body dualism, which even exclusive materialists
must concede to be at least conceivable*, there is
already available the intelligible postulate, understood within the human experience, of mind as a centre
of consciousness and irreducible intentionality and
whose manifestations are not to be identified with
brain processes, nevertheless producing effects in the
realm of matter. If in our experience, mind, of an

---

*   Some have objected, as Antony Quinton points out (Quinton, 1973, p. 319), that mental and bodily events as postulated
by dualists are too dissimilar to be sensibly conceived as mutually interacting. And Hume required that causes and effects must be
contiguous in space and time, thereby ruling dualism's mental
events out of the field of possible causal efficacy. But as
Quinton observes, such views 'should be discarded as the mistaken
product of a myopically partial viewpoint, concentrated on the
physical world'. He does not in the end support dualism and
thinks that 'mental events appear to be idle' which is, he thinks,
the real difficulty of the postulate of mind-body interaction.
But our concern here is merely to show the conceivability of the
interaction, and with that, the conceivability of divine interaction with the natural realm.

order of phenomena conceivably unique and distinct from matter, and in its most crucially distinct manifestations in purposiveness is to be explained in terms of motive and reason rather than of causal determination, does as a matter of fact bring about effects in physical nature; surely this suffices to give sense to the conception of a divine mind, postulated to be likewise intentional and rational, though supremely so, effecting occurrences in the natural realm? If two essentially distinct orders of existence, one material and the other not so, within the natural realm can be intelligibly envisaged to be effectively interacting, can it be utterly unintelligible for us to conceive a transcendent God's effective agency in the natural realm? So too, since in our experience, minds do, or at least may be conceived to interact with other minds, can it be utterly senseless to talk of the divine mind interacting with human minds, and vice-versa?

Now any deficiency there may be in our above arguments will be remedied (and this is the definitive answer we mentioned at the start) by our case in Part Two for the intelligibility of the concept of miracles and of the ascertaining of miraculous occurences (pp. 73 - 99). For if miracles, conceived as violations of natural laws through divine agency, make sense and may possibly even be ascertained, then it only follows that it makes sense to talk of incorporeal divine personhood and God's agency within the natural realm. We will argue that in special religious contexts, certain coincidences of religiously significant events could sensibly be explained only in terms of divine intention and agency. Those contexts and circumstances would therefore, for our present concern, provide the substantive experiential basis for our claims to the conceivability of incorporeal transcendent personhood, anlogous to human persons in terms at least of effective agency and intentionality.

(ii)   the Problem of Evil

The next hurdle facing us is to show that despite the fact of evil, the postulate of an omnipotent God who is all-good is not internally incoherent. This problem crops up even within religious schools of thought that do not obviously postulate divine personal agency. Even ignoring the universalistic interpretation of world religions suggested above (according to which no religion is totally unimplicated by the doctrines of other religions and even impersonal conceptions of ultimate being would merely be stressing one facet or emphasis of the personal deity), A.C. Ewing has suggested (Ewing, 1973, p. 236) that the utter commitment and trust required in all religious worship presupposes the belief that in the last analysis, reality, or the destiny of persons and the universe, is good, and therefore that any ultimately unexplained evil must mar this cosmic picture that alone can justify our religious awe and reverence.

Now the many attempts at providing a theodicy and the sorts of objections they have provoked are well-known (see Mackie, 1971, for a comprehensive presentation). I want however to argue that many of the objections, even though pertinent when we consider the claims to full adequacy that were made for those theodicies, can be seen, on a revised account of the theodicies that present them as providing mere inklings in human terms of what the divine explanation of evil might be, to be imposing too stringently, by their not appreciating those inklings, ordinary language semantic criteria on religious discourse in their implied demand for a full theodicy in human terms. And as regards the theodicy that seeks to explain moral evil (evil ascribable to moral agency other than divine agency) by reference to the purported free-will of moral agents other than God, I shall show not only that it is a suggestive inkling of an explanation of moral evil, but also that it is likewise indicative of a divine explanation of evil that is not due to human choices. The upshot of all this (especially, as we shall suggest, when the case is put alongside our arguments in the next part that show the initial plausibility of, and the possibility of confirming, religious truth-claims) will be that religion is not necessarily conceptually incoherent despite evil, since those inklings the theodicies provide should constitute the minimal sense in human terms which is necessary, by our criterion of minimal intelligibility stated earlier (p. 2), to warrant the suspending of our disbelief in God despite evil, pending further testings, on whatever available independent grounds, of religious truth-claims. For if God could be believed in on independent grounds, then religious belief would not be incoherent despite evil, in view of the conceivability of an adequate divine theodicy.

First, let us make the general and for our purpose crucial observation, that all that a theodicy need provide is sufficient indication of a possible explana-

34

tion of evil, and not anything approaching an adequate solution. For if God and his 'transcendent' state of being exist, even though fundamentally but not in all respects inconceivable in human terms, and man's eternal state of being after death is likewise inconceivable in terms of present human experience, then this must be the perspective within which the problem of evil, which is essentially one that arises within the confines of human language and experience, should be viewed. Therefore any consideration as to the adequacy of a theodicy must be done with due cognisance taken of the necessary limitations of human language and perspective for the enterprise. Now theodicies that <u>merely</u> appeal to divine mystery, and admonish the believer in religion to have faith that there is an answer to the problem even though it is presently unavailable to human understanding, have rightly been rejected. For such theodicies amount to an attempt to totally shelve a difficulty which threatens the very possibility of our intelligibly asserting theism. To continue to say that God or ultimate reality is supremely good, in the face of some of the baser atrocities of natural and moral evil, would be to so empty the term 'good' of meaning that 'God is good' can't even be asserted, <u>unless</u> some plausible indications are also given to show that it is conceivable, necessarily in human terms, that there could be a divine solution to the problem. And we said before that the doctrine of revelation itself implies some ability on our part to understand divine truths (Cf. p. 2). But nothing more than initial indications of the conceivability of a divine solution should be expected, considering the transcendent and eternal perspective within which human lives and present suffering will have to be viewed, assuming religion is true. For then it could possibly be the case that only 'heaven knows' how the anguish men and animals undergo might somehow fit into an overall fabric and seen, in the ultimate perspective, to be logically necessary for worthwhile ends. I think if we view many of the theodicies that have been proffered as such mere indications for the sceptic to suspend disbelief pending grounds for belief which may be elsewhere available, and not as attempts at the logically impossible, i.e. a solution given in terms of human experience, they will emerge successful enough for our purpose. I don't mean theodicies that go back on the claim that God is almighty, or which deny the reality of evil, or say that the sense of 'good' as applied to God need not have an adequate minimal symmetry with the sense of 'good' in human language. To deny that God is almighty would be to 'solve' the problem by abandoning the concept of God, and anyhow the utter trust and commitment religions require would be inappropriate before a limited God. The Judaeo-Christian tradition asserts the reality of evil from which deliverance and salvation is promised, and in-as-far as oriental religions like Hinduism, Buddhism and Taoism can be interpreted to really deny the reality of suffering, they are to that extent denying a known fact (but see p. 8 above). Anyhow, the view that suffering is an illusion or merely an aspect of the good implies that, while it lasts, the illusion or aspect is experienced and suffered, and the existence of this conscious state would suffice to mar the picture of the ultimate goodness of things if unexplained. As regards theodicies that want not at all to subject God's purported goodness to evaluation on man's criteria, we need only to refer back to our assertion of the minimal sense religious tenets must have in human terms.

Rather I have in mind theodicies that make some effort, necessarily in terms of human experience and language, to accommodate the fact of evil within the fabric of the religious viewpoint. Examples are arguments such as that good cannot exist without evil, or that evil is necessary as a counterpart to good; that evil is necessary as a means to good; that the universe is better with some evil in it than it would be if there were no evil; and that evil is due to human or other created moral agents' free will. Mackie, in the paper referred to, discusses these theodicies under the heading 'fallacious solutions' and he sets these against the sort of theodicies we mentioned above which he calls, sarcastically, 'adequate solutions', their adequacy being only in their tacit denial that there is a problem to solve since, as Mackie points out, 'the problem will not arise if one gives up at least one of the propositions that constitute it', (p. 93) i.e. the proposition that God is almighty, or that he is all good, or that evil is real. A virtue of the 'fallacious solutions' is therefore in that being 'fallacious' they must at least be attempted solutions rather than evasions, the attempts being necessarily made in terms of observations from within the human experience. We will now see that some of these attempts, if not singly then collectively, present enough 'this-worldly' inklings of the issue to enable us to suspend our disbelief in religion despite the presence of evil, and to render it reasonable for us to cultivate the faith to believe, should we have independent reasons for belief

36

in God, that there is a divine solution to the problem
of evil even though it is presently still a mystery to
us. I contend further that the 'fallaciousness' of the
attempts - necessarily judged so on the basis of this-
worldly experience and criteria - far from invalidating
the theodicies, really strengthens them once they can
be shown to succeed in providing the sufficient minimal
explanation of evil to enable us to suspend disbelief
in the way indicated. For firstly, we should expect
much of religious tenets to be in human terms ultimately inexplicable and mysterious if religion were true.
Secondly, as regards the problem of evil, some of the
more abject evils, whether or not they are due to evil
choices, appear within the human perspective so callous
and cruel that it would be contradictory, indeed immoral and irreligious, to envisage a full solution of the
problem of evil given in terms of human experience.
While the believer, as we will argue, must have the
faith to believe that a solution ultimately exists in
terms that <u>transcend</u> human experience and understanding
(since there are sufficient 'inklings' and analogies in
the human experience to warrant this suspension of
rationality), he must while in his present natural life
appreciate fully the strain the problem of evil places
on his beliefs (since he is nonetheless inescapably a
'prisoner' of the natural order, where with all the
rationality he is capable of, he must find suffering
ultimately unexplained). Failure to do so would put
him in danger of becoming immune to suffering, due to
a too ready willingness to dismiss it as justifiable
and reconcilable with good, a practice that is <u>inhuman</u>
in our present perspective of things. And part of the
mystery the problem of evil poses for the believer is
precisely the question how it could be the case that a
problem, which in the final analysis is <u>irresolvable</u>
<u>when viewed from the human perspective</u>, could ultimate-
ly have a solution in the divine perspective. The
religious practice that this paradox should result in
is to, like Christ, do all one could to alleviate
human and animal suffering while having the faith to
believe that all things, including present suffering,
somehow, beyond our intelligibility, in the end 'work
together for good'.

Now, within the human experience, it is true
that evil aids in the appreciation of good, say as a
foil for it; or that virtues like courage and endurance, or mercy, could not exist in the absence of
suffering to endure, or a fallen foe to spare; or that
without evil, great human achievements like Shakespear-

ian tragedies and the artistic and moral successes they
represent could never be. And there is sense in the
contention that a universe where such moral and aesthetic goods are achievable and achieved would still be
better than one free from evil but where such goods
cannot exist. (A very persuasive theodicy made along
these lines may be found in Ewing, 1973, Chapter 9).
We can also make some sense of the 'Irenean theodicy'
advanced by John Hick (Hick, 1966, Part 4), in which
evil is explained in terms of the necessity for God to
be veiled from his creation in order to maintain 'the
epistemic distance' between God and man purported to
be necessary for man's soul-making (pp. 332-3). For
provided that God's presence would in fact be so overwhelming as to render it impossible in practice for man
to know he exists without also being irresistibly
drawn towards him in response and love, it would be
understandable that to enable man's _free_ response to
God in faith and love,which is envisaged to be essential in his soul-making, it must not be obvious from
observing his creation that God exists; whatever reasons for belief available should therefore be given
only to those who have begun by their own initiative
to 'seek'. And indeed both moral and natural evil
suggest positively that God doesn't exist, thus conceivably functioning to strengthen the 'veil of ignorance'
separating man from God.

I think however that it is essential, for the
potency of such theodicies, to recognise that they fail
as final and complete solutions to the problem; and to
claim only that they are, if not in themselves sufficient pointers, within the human experience, to enable
the suspension of disbelief referred to above, then
sufficient for the purpose, in view of the possibility
and availability (as we will show in the next part)
of our having some evidences favourable to religious
belief, which will render it to that degree easier and
more rational to suspend disbelief. Now as a final
solution, which necessarily must be conceived and
formulated in the terms of natural experience, such
theodicies must fail. For example, against them it
has been objected that there have been instances of
human and animal suffering that, from all we know in
the human experience, seem inconceivable as being
designed to help build up anybody's moral courage and
endurance. Much animal pain takes place,say, in the
depth of jungles where men do not exist for their
sympathies, say, to be evoked. Also, it seems a strain
on our imagination to envisage large-scale natural

catastrophes, in which whole populations, and in time, perhaps whole civilisations, have been wiped out, as being designed to strengthen moral virtues. Certainly in sudden deaths as a result, say, of earthquakes, the moral virtues of the victims themselves, many of whom must be babes in arms, aren't being cultivated. And the multitudes of actual and possible unknown victims of such natural calamities must or will have perished in vain without even the mere possibility of being occasions for other persons' soul-making. In any case, why so much pain? Why not a little less (what difference would that extra hour of throbbing pain, say, in a cancer patient make, since whether his courage and endurance would be successfully tested must have already been decided after the lingering months or years?), and why should not the remaining pains be already sufficient for whatever soul-making that is envisaged? (See Puccetti, 1967, p. 262). As regards Hick's Irenean theodicy, we may ask if it is really necessary for God, in order to maintain the 'epistemic distance' between himself and man, to tolerate the endurance of so much suffering by his creatures, since even a universe which is free from suffering would merely mean religion is freed from a major obstacle to belief in it, rather than that a positive reason then exists for belief. The absence of 'flaws' in the universe could be merely a happy coincidence and would not in itself constitute convincing or even merely positive evidence of divine purpose. Or, granted that so much evil as man in fact suffers is logically necessary for some moral and aesthetic goods to actualise, it may still be asked whether it is really worthwhile to have such goods at the expense of having so much evil. Anyhow, are all such goods absolute and intrinsic goods, or are some at least merely relative goods that are parasitic on the circumstances wherein they arise; like the virtue of showing mercy to a fallen foe, or of courage in the face of danger and suffering. In the latter case, they would not be goods any longer when the evil circumstances that occasion them are eliminated. And then the universe free from the evil would not be worse off in respect of the absence of those relative goods. Indeed it might be better off not needing those 'goods' which would not be goods anymore in any case. Most surely, it would be better off without some of such 'goods' and also some of the more abject of evils that occasion them. And as regards some at least of the evils which are not logically necessary to the ascertainment of goods but which nonethelsss do result in future goods, we may ask whether they would really be

redeemed on account of the resultant goods. Don't we,
in human experience, censure abject cruelty and the
like as intrinsically bad irrespective of whatever
goods they may result in? And an almighty God who can
do all that is logically possible should have enabled
mankind to attain those goods otherwise.

Now the sort of objections exemplified above
succeed to show merely that not all suffering can be
explained in the respective ways concerned. There
surely are occasions within the human experience where
we indeed rightly think, say, that some pains are
worthwhile enduring for the sake of a better appreciation of certain goods, or for the attaining of logically or otherwise resultant goods. For instance, I
should not envy, say, a millionaire's play-boy son for
his trouble-free life but should regard the moderate
trials of life I have had to endure and overcome from
time to time as worthwhile experiences for the making
of the relatively seasoned character I am. The initially seeming injustice of it all would rightly seem
to me now to be really a privilege, judged in the
present better perspective of my past. I am as the
result better equipped for the future challenges of
life, with its risks and pains to avoid or endure,
without which life would be somewhat thinned and sim-
plified. Now I think that such experiential bases for
explaining some at least of evils should suffice, especially in view of our case in Part Two for the possibility of our having independent grounds for theism,
to render unduly dogmatic the rejection of religion on
account of the purported internal incoherence owing to
the presence of evil. If some of a class of phenomena
can already be satisfactorily explained in terms of
human experience, then surely it is premature and
unduly dogmatic to rule out as inconceivable a possible
divine solution to the other unexplained members of
that class; in view of the conceivability and practical
possibility, to be demonstrated in Part Two, of our
having independent rational grounds for theism, the
realising of which would render it rationally obligatory, vis-a-vis the transcendent, that we accept, indeed expect, that ultimately there will be things unexplained and mysterious. If it be objected that the
abject and problematic evils do not, by that very description of them, belong to the same class of phenomena as those sufferings that we can explain, we can
readily concede that and still have our case. For
surely the two purported sorts of phenomena would still
be similar in respects significant enough for our con-

tention that once one sort could be explained, this
should be the experiential basis to warrant our conceiving a divine explanation for the other, in the
special circumstances surrounding this particular
issue.

Let me stress that the impossibility of explaining, on the same experiential bases, the abject
and humanly unexplainable evils, without stretching
too much the ordinary meanings of terms like 'good'
and 'evil', could after all be a necessary impossibility within the human experience, if religion is true.
This is a point worth remembering every time we retort
with regard to the more excruciating and lingering
pains: 'But how is it ever conceivable that this would
in the ultimate perspective of things work towards the
good?' or 'Whatever the good consequences, wouldn't
such be still unredeemed bad? They are so in the human
experience'. Now the moral repugnance so expressed is
quite in order in the human experience, and indeed I
suggested that it is a very consistent 'religious'
sentiment. It promotes compassion and Christlikeness.
We should go along with it and do the only thing humans
must do under the circumstances and having the only
perspective they have ultimately to view these things,
i.e. alleviate such suffering unreservedly within the
present life. But we should all the same never forget
that this repugnance against the evils concerned, and
the inconceivability to us of their ever having a
purpose and being somehow transformed to good, is an
inconceivability seen only within the human perspective.
However unable we are in practice and principle to
detach ourselves from our experience and language as
humans (we have in such matters reached the limits of
our world), we must always leave room for the theoretical possibility, that passes our understanding, of
the evils being transformed in the divine perspective.
For the human perspective would have necessary limitations, which our involvement and 'imprisonment' within
the human situation would logically prevent our realisation of, and even within the human perspective there
are some evils which are quite adequately explained in
terms of the goods they enable. Like a child who,
while the suffering lasts, cannot as yet see how that
will help to harden him into the intrinsically worthwhile, self-respecting, courageous man he will become,
so within the human perspective we may lack the experience and language to comprehend what the ultimate answer to suffering might be. We have to admit that an
'adequate' solution is ultimately unintelligible to us

41

and yet avoid disbelieving religion merely on this account, since there is this analogy, and other inklings available in human experience, to warrant this, and since, as we said, an independent case can be envisaged in positive support of religion, which will render it the more reasonable, in view of all that has been argued, to allow the appeal to divine mystery in explaining the problem. In other words, while it is unintelligible to us that all evil may be justified, it is intelligible to us that this human unintelligibility might in divine terms be ultimately intelligible.

Now, we have not yet considered the free-will theodicy. I have left this till now because it needs a more detailed mention.

the free-will theodicy

The free-will theodicy is essentially the contention that evil is the result of evil choices which God cannot prevent without infringing on the free will of created moral agents. It asserts that the creation of autonomous moral agents is an end worthwhile in itself and the universe is the better having such agents per se notwithstanding the evils or goods that have consequently arisen. (It does not need to assert, as Antony Flew seems to think, that the goods consequent upon free-will far outweigh the evils. Flew's contention that this assertion is in principle impossible to prove is therefore irrelevant to the validity of the theodicy. See Flew 1973, pp. 232, 3). It is commonly thought that at most this theodicy can, if successful, only account for what is commonly regarded as moral evil; but I think it can conceivably account also for what is usually regarded as natural evil. Now it would indeed be implausible to claim, as some did, that man's moral choices could have had repercussions in physical and biological nature such that the order of creation could have been spoilt by man's sins, thus resulting in diseases and the like. Natural catastrophes, disease in animals, and the pains and cruelty caused by one animal preying upon another were existent prior to man. Anyhow the whole idea is pointless from the point of view of the free will theodicy, for it is surely not necessary, for the preserving of man's autonomy, to extend his environment for effective agency (without which environment autonomy would of course be inconceivable) so far as to affect even the constitution of physical and biological nature.

But the case is different where it is envisaged, as C.S. Lewis has somewhat done (Lewis, 1940, pp. 121-124), that there could have been created non-natural, 'spiritual' beings, such as angels and fallen angels, whose effective moral agency, because they have been given God-like powers for purposes beyond our ken, indeed extend into the natural realm to either enhance God's creation there or spoil it. In this light, what to us are natural evils could be the result of the evil choices of such supernatural 'principalities and powers' which, for the maximisation of good, God could not have prevented, since to do so would mean not actualising those free moral agents. This conjecture should not be lightly dismissed and caricatured as the summoning up of devils - 'calling up evil spirits' - to the rescue of an ailing theodicy, in the manner of Antony Flew (Flew, 1966, p. 55). For, as we suggested when discussing the intelligibility of incorporeal and transcendent personal existence, if we accept that men exist, as centres of awareness and agency not to be identified with merely overt behaviour and bodily processes, effecting changes through the material medium (Cf. pp. 28-33), what is so ludicrous in the conjecture itself that supernatural minds also exist interacting, perhaps through 'spiritual' media, and also through natural media, and having powers and an environment for effective agency far more extensive than man's? Be it noted that the conjecture has the support of most religious orthodoxies, and traditionally had set a stage for moral drama far more complex and cosmic in significance than the post scientific morality of merely lonesome men in mutual interaction in an exclusively naturalistic, single-layer cosmos. The issue is really whether there are grounds for the conjecture, keeping in mind Occam's razor. But here we are merely concerned with the <u>conceivability</u> of the free will theodicy being a general theodicy accounting also for what, from man's viewpoint, appear as natural evil.

Now, <u>given the assumption</u> that the universe with its moral agents, both natural ones <u>and the envisaged transnatural ones</u>, having <u>the extent</u> of freedom and <u>scope</u> for agency they in fact have or are envisaged to have, together with <u>all</u> the evil that has occurred and will occur as a consequence of this, would be still better than any other envisaged universe where the same moral agents exist but with <u>less scope</u> for freedom and consequently commit less evil, the free will theodicy could <u>conceivably</u> be, even from the human perspective, quite adequate. However, I shall show that the assump-

43

tion is questionable. The upshot will be that, like the other theodicies that <u>somewhat</u> explain evil without doing the theologically inept and logically impossible task of explaining it totally in human terms, the free-will theodicy, is in the end still dubious.

Now our identity as moral agents could surely be preserved in a universe where enough scope for free-will exists but with that much less scope for it as would reduce somewhat or perhaps even all the amount of suffering accruing from it.

It is surely conceivable that God determines only that evil,or excessive evil, cannot be chosen, and leaves men free to choose between varying degrees of good and moral neutrality or some not-so-hurtful evils. Discussion by philosophers on the issue has so far been conducted as if moral freedom involves only two choices, for evil or for good, and that if there is to be free choice at all, choice for the bad <u>must</u> be allowed. But surely moral agents also choose between, say, the better or best, the less good or morally neutral. The point therefore is whether being able to choose the bad or the excessively bad is essential for beings to qualify as persons, and also whether, after being deprived of the choice for, say, too much evil, there would still remain enough scope for moral free-dom, among the possible choices left. Regarding the former question, we may observe that surely it is the freedom to have enough choices, rather than the ability to choose in one particular direction that is essential to the person-concept. True, there would be no scope, say, for moral repugnance and righteous anger against evil, or perhaps for showing mercy to a fallen foe. But then, anger and moral repugnance could be brought against, say, choices which could have been better. And there would still be scope for the sort of goodwill that makes merciful acts praiseworthy, like going the second mile with someone. At any rate, there is hard-ly the need to eliminate <u>all</u> evil, for surely it is the excessively evil and <u>painful</u> that really pose the pro-blem of evil for the theist. The milder pains could quite plausibly be explained, say, as trials along the 'soul-making' process.* There could then be some scope

---

* True, this distinction between 'milder' pains and 'ex-cessive' pains is hard to demarcate in practice, and from the human perspective, some relativity or subjectivity would enter here to blur the boundary. But surely God can be left to do the conceivable, and he who knows all would know where the boundary

44

for moral repugnance even against evil. Regarding the question as to the scope left for freedom, it should be remembered that in the human situation, there already are natural inhibitions to acts like voluntarily stopping to breathe. What we need envisage is more of such natural checks so that too much evil could not be chosen. If human life, as we know it, is such that the sort of inhibitions to freedom already exist, who is to arbitrarily claim that once that much more of such inhibitions are envisaged, beings in the situation would no longer be persons?

Two possible objections, first suggested by Ninian Smart (Smart, 1961), may be levelled at our position. One is that words like 'good' and 'bad' in our conjectured world would take on a different meaning and this would threaten our very conception of moral agency. The other is that in such postulates, logical possibility is not enough and that sufficient details should be given to provide a sufficiently meaningful description of the sort of world envisaged. Regarding the first point, it is of course true that there would be an upward meaning-shift along the scale of degrees of good and bad, such that what is now, say, least good might be regarded as bad in the conjectured world. But surely the sort of consequential linguistic shifts in our postulate would not affect the basic sense of moral terms, which surely is in valuations as to what in any world is regarded as praiseworthy or blameworthy. So, it may be asked: why stick to a bad form of life just in order to preserve the representative language? To the other objection, might we not retort again that since God is almighty, he could quite rightly be left to do the not logically impossible, even though man is yet unable to describe the details of the postulate? In any case, we have already given some hints as to the sort of biological or mental inhibitions man could have been born with which could render impossible his making bad or excessively bad choices. And the differences, say, in moral institutions and conceptions, and in language, wouldn't be too difficult to envisage.

---

objectively should be. That the distinction is conceivable is sufficiently evidenced by the fact that we can point to some specific though extreme exemplifications of 'excessive' painful experiences, like a cancer patient having to linger on in pain for another week, or day, or hour, after having been already two years in that condition, which can be removed without really upsetting the preconditions for the moral freedom of persons. (I have in mind Stanley Paluch's criticism of my view, which first appeared in a

It would seem,therefore, that the free will
theodicy could not be fully adequate from the human
viewpoint. However, if it can be successfully contended that it is, even if only conceivably, a logical
contradiction to envisage the universe of moral agents
being free and yet without having to suffer some at
least of the evils that have in fact arisen or will
arise as the result of human free choices, then the
free-will theodicy would be suggestive of a possible
hidden divine purpose for both what we regard as moral
and natural evils. For this would suffice to render it
intelligible, within the human perspective, to conceive
a possible analogous set of circumstances in the divine
and eternal perspective, where for some like redeeming
factors unknown to man, the giving of free-will to man
and transnatural moral agents has necessitated all of
those 'moral' and natural' evils in the world. After
all, since that much evil in man's perspective is
already conceivably accountable in terms of man's free-
will, it should surely be expected that in God's perspective, which would include purposes beyond our ken,
much more evil may on similar grounds be accountable.
And God's perspective would include the extent of freedom our postulated transnatural moral agents would need
and the expectedly much greater possibility for evil
this could involve. It might even be the case that
this freedom would include power over natural minds,
producing co-evil-doers like Hitler, whose scope for
freedom and evil seemed in the human perspective way
beyond the necessity of human moral agency. In other
words, we would get the adequately suggestive theodicy
- one that would satisfy the minimal 'conceivability in
human terms' criterion to enable our suspension of disbelief despite evil -. that for some conjecturable even
though in fact humanly unknown and unknowable reasons,
having those free moral agents with nothing less than
the scope for freedom they now have in the universe is
still the best situation possible, all the consequent
pains notwithstanding.

Now, we said above that moral agents could conceivably still retain their personal status, with evil
or excessive evil due to evil choices being eliminated,
since there would in that situation still be sufficient
scope for moral choice. Nevertheless it is also

---

paper: see Paluch, 1976; Tan, 1974)

conceivable, for it is not implausible and certainly intelligible, to maintain that the range of possible choices minimally required for moral agency must include some possibility for bad choices. It might plausibly be argued that restricting moral choices to merely degrees of good and moral neutrality, which we allowed for above as a logical possibility, would in fact water down the substantive significance of the moral life too much, despite our contention above that in the resultant upward meaning shift on our scale of praise and blame in a world where evil choices are totally elimated, these moral concepts would still have their basic functions. 'Moral agents' in the envisaged condition would therefore tend to be too experientially discontinuous from what we now understand of the term. Now if even from the human perspective the total eliminating of the possibility for bad choices could already mean a somewhat extreme thinning of men's moral experience that threatens its defacto recognisability, isn't it therefore conceivable that in God's perspective some essentials to the moral life beyond man's understanding and appreciation are so similarly bound up with the actual extent of moral evil in the universe (which would include what in the human perspective is seen as 'natural' evil, if we bear in mind our postulate of the possible effects of the moral agency of created transnatural beings) that it would be impossible for God to both have the intrinsic good of created moral beings and also the elimination of what to us are evils beyond the necessity of **moral freedom?** In other words, this conceivable necessity of at least some evil choices being possible in the world as a prerequisite to having free persons (including our envisaged transnatural ones) surely provides us the basis for our further envisaging, for unknown reasons, an analogical fully comprehensive cosmic theodicy.

There are however in recent philosophy of religion two much-discussed objections to the freewill theodicy that directly oppose the above conclusion. First, J. L. Mackie (Mackie, 71) seems to have argued that God in his foreknowledge could have actualised only the subset of possible moral beings whom he had foreseen would only choose the right, and so it is logically possible, and therefore morally obligatory, for an almighty and good God to have done so, and thus to have created only moral beings who could possibly have chosen the bad and yet freely refrained from doing so. Secondly, Antony Flew has developed his early critique of the theodicy (Flew, 1955) into an explicit 'compatibility thesis' (Flew, 1973), which takes the 'soft determinist' approach of purporting to reconcile the notion of human free will with that of God's pre-arranging that the moral beings he has created would always choose the good. An implication of Flew's contention is that it is not crucial for the notion of free moral agency that there must be really possible alternative choices. The upshot is that even a fully determined 'choice' could still be 'free', and therefore it is not necessary, in the creation of moral persons, to allow for a range for possible choice. The success of this thesis would of course upset the freewill theodicy, and also my version of it, since both presuppose the denial of Flew's conclusion.

First, let us discuss Mackie's suggestion by reference to a recent restatement of it by Stanley Paluch, (1973). The thesis is that God's bringing about a moral utopia could be conceived as his knowing in advance which of his proposed creatures would freely choose the good consistently, and his actualising only such persons in the conjectured utopia: 'we need only imagine God actualising that proper-subset of possible human beings which would correspond to the beings in our Cosmomorphic Utopia' (p. 91).

Now, I shall later question the assumption tacit in this argument that omnipotence should be capable of foreseeing even the actual free choices of would-be moral agents. In so doing, I shall be attacking the thesis more fundamentally. Here, let us give it this assumption and see that despite this, it is untenable. Now the postulate verges on absurdities. But first, let us indicate possible moral objections to it. Now, there is a difference between (1) God's not wanting to create moral beings from the start, and (2) God's wanting to create them, seeing into the future to get a preview of the would-be persons, and then deciding not to actualise some persons. Regarding the latter, various questions could be raised casting doubts on divine goodness. In the human situation, practices like abortion and contraception may be plausibly argued to be unlike murder, on the ground that nothing quite like a person exists as yet in the pregnancy to be terminated or prevented. Practices like euthanasia are justifiable on grounds such as that they are the least amongst evils. Paluch's conception is, however, of God seeing into the future moral situation of would-be persons, getting quite intimately acquainted with them (in order to see their every moral choice and their motives, both conscious and unconscious), and then deciding that a huge (necessarily) subset of the multitudes of such personalities should not actualise! Would such an act be justifiable on the ground that it is the least among evils? But isn't God omnipotent enough not to be thus cornered? (We have seen that an utopia of persons, where excessive moral evil is absent, is conceivable, without recourse to Paluch's hideous postulate.)

Another such objection to the postulate has initially to do with the question of justice, but it then develops into a conceptual objection. There need be no neat division between the morally good and bad. For instance, the presence of good people might be the reason for others choosing the bad, just as the activities of bad people might be the very impetus necessary for some others to counteract by being good. Now, Paluch envisages that would-be persons who would not choose evil should be actualised; but would it be just for God to do this when it was also foreseen that without some good people, many bad ones, not to be actualised, would not choose the bad? Perhaps this fact would not absolve the bad from blame, and certainly the good shouldn't consequently be also blamed. But what should be done to those would-be good people who were foreseen to abandon the good in some respect or other as a consequence of the would-be bad people not actualising? Would they, because of this, be justly considered as the would-be bad? Generally, it could be that, except perhaps for the exceptionally evil man, most people, who some time or other in their life-time make morally bad choices, do so in such a socially inter-dependent manner that the blame on them might be so small in the sight of an all-seeing God as to render it unjust for them not to be actualised while those, who merely happen to make, consciously or not, the right choices got the chance to live. Even if the cumulative evil caused were colossal, each man viewed individually might contribute just a little to it. And perhaps with some rather than all such persons not actualised, the remainders might no longer choose evil. But not actualising only such some persons would raise questions such as why those persons and not some other would-be 'bad' persons, whose absence might have similar results. Not actualising all under such circumstances would of course continue to put divine goodness in doubt.

Similar considerations will show the conjecture to be absurd. For instance, there might have to be an infinite regress of instances of divine foreseeing. The initial foresight would tell who not to actualise, a second would be needed to tell who would not remain good once those were not actualised, a third would be needed to tell who else would not remain good once those spotted in the second foresight were not actualised, and so on. Assuming that the regress could end somewhere with every foreseen person remaining good despite the absence of the successive groups, there might be too few left to actualise in order to make the human race. After all, isn't it said that in the world as we have it 'there is none righteousness, no not one'? Another sort of conceptual difficulty is evident once we look at the conjecture from the genealogical viewpoint. Not actualising morally evil persons would surely cause breaks in the genealogy of every good person who was to be actualised. As such, the entire biological structure of humanity would have to be drastically changed so as to implement the plan. Would they still be persons if they were, say, moulded and made and then blown to life, like Adam? If so, would they be the same persons as those foreseen?

Many more such objections could of course be thought out against the postulate, and we have given a fair sample. The upshot of this is that the Mackie-Paluch conjecture is a logically impossible feat for a good and almighty God, since it involves the immoral and absurd. It therefore fails to debunk the free will theodicy. We now proceed to discuss the second objection, which is Antony Flew's 'compatibility thesis'.

Flew's thesis is: (1) that we must in giving a sense to 'free will' regard only the ordinary language sense of 'free', since ordinary language is the context wherein 'free' gets its meaning and any other purported sense would be arbitrary, stipulative and irrelevant; (2) that the ordinary use of 'free' is at least theory-neutral as regards the free-will versus determinism controversy, it being used merely to distinguish ordinary behavioural manifestations picked out by such phrases as 'my jumping out of the window' from those by phrases like 'my being thrown out of the window'; and it is therefore non-committal as to whether or not freedom should be given the 'libertarian' sense of 'free (unconstrained)', since irrespective of the outcome of this theoretical controversy, those behavioural situations picked out by the two sorts of phrases will continue to exist to give 'free' its ordinary use and sense; (3) that in fact there are ample linguistic evidences to show that in the ordinary sense of 'free',constrained actions are still 'free', since their respective agents could have done otherwise than they did despite the constraints - a bank manager under constraint by robbers to hand over the cash or die could have chosen to die; (4) that in fact in ordinary language, only those of our behaviour which are 'constrained' by our character and nature, such that they issue from and are compatible with it, are rightly regarded as acts that are ours for which we are to be held responsible; (5) that therefore God could be conceived, without infringing on our ordinary use of 'free', to have created man with a certain nature, and to have placed certain specific constraints in his environment, so that given that nature and those constraints, man would still choose, but in each case always choose the right; (6) that anyhow the doctrines of creation, omnipotence and free-will imply the consistency of saying both that 'without (God) was not anything made that was made' (meaning, presumably, that even human natures, our wills and free choices have been created by God), and that man has free will; and (7) that in any case, assuming the truth of the doctrine of creation as understood in terms of God's being creatively responsible for even our minutest decisions and acts, or the truth of some psychological conjecture such as that all our behaviour, even what we ordinarily regard to be voluntary, is really determined in the sense that we could not have chosen to behave otherwise, our ordinary senses of 'free' and 'unfree', in reference to the distinction between the two sorts of behaviour described under 2 above, would still retain the same use to sort out those behavioural manifestations; therefore 'free' in this sense, which is the theoretically unbiased sense, would be compatible with even a thoroughly deterministic universe, as long as the two sorts of behaviour remain to be marked out by the terms 'free' and 'unfree'; and remain these surely would, since no theorising on free will and determinism would affect the 'known facts' that there are 'motions' on the one hand (like a man being thrown out of the window), and 'movings' on the other (like a man jumping out of the window). Flew concedes though, as regards the latter, that the significance with which we would regard the distinction, and the notions of moral responsibility, praise and blame, would be reduced considerably in a totally deterministic universe, but he curiously still insists that 'free' would in the eventuality still retain its present ordinary use.

Now it is surely untrue that the ordinary use
of 'free' is theory-neutral. Flew has himself conceded this in saying, in point 7 above, that the significance of the distinction between the two 'sorts' of
behaviour would be reduced drastically should total
determinism be true; for surely the significance we
presently accord the distinction is connected to our
theoretical presuppositions as regards the behaviours
concerned. True, constrained <u>actions</u> are still somewhat voluntary and should be distinguished from such
behavioural motions as our being thrown out of the
window. But notice that we would excuse the bank manager in Flew's illustration for choosing to hand over
the money to the robber rather than be killed only
because there is no other choice open to him, and the
choice to die, we think, would under the circumstances
be unreasonable. This shows that constrained actions
are in ordinary language regarded as being to that
extent less free, and as such the moral responsibility
ascribed to such constrained moral agents would accor-
dingly be reduced. True too, we would blame a well-
trained secret agent (another illustration of Flew's)
for choosing to save his own life when under the constraints of torture and as the result betrayed his com-
rades. But this is because his training had presumably
made him brave enough to choose to die, so that this
had become for him a really viable alternative act.
Notice again that we would not blame, or at least not
blame to the same extent as we would the secret agent,
an untrained frightened village woman who under torture
did the same. For her 'action', though she may <u>appear</u>
to have chosen it, had presumably been determined by
overwhelming and compelling fear, and therefore her
behaviour is treated more as motion, like her being
thrown out of the window. Flew himself need not deny
all this, since his examples are meant only to show
that a free act is not necessarily a totally unconstrained act. All the same, his own examples bring out
our point that far from being theory-neutral, the class
of behaviour the word 'free' distinguishes is to be
understood in terms of the theory that a really voluntary act must involve the presence of at least one
other viable alternative act, such that the agent could
really have chosen that alternative, there being no
causally sufficient antecedent conditions that had
determined the choice that was made. (It may be objected that the latter cannot be ordinarily meant by 'free
choice' since we can never prove the condition to be

satisfied; and that all that the term is used to mean is that the ordinarily recognisable impediments to actions are absent, and this leaves room for a wider, metaphysical determinism. But my point is precisely that this ordinary condition of the use of 'free' has point in terms of the free will theory, it being ordinarily assumed that <u>nothing else</u> besides those ordinarily recognisable impediments may hinder our free acts. This is why assuming it was demonstrated that even our ordinarily-regarded 'free' acts are really determined, our concept of freedom, as Flew recognises, would be drastically reduced in significance.) And the wider the range of available alternatives, the greater will be the moral agent's accountability for having chosen the way he has.

Now this notion of 'free' acts is all the proponents of free will need be committed to, although Flew in point <u>2</u> wants to commit them to proposing 'free (unconstrained)'. This then gives him the leeway he needs for point <u>4</u>, which is a key point of contention of the compatibilist; namely that only actions which are <u>constrained</u> by a person's character and nature, such that they issue from and are compatible with them, are really and recognisably that person's actions. But we may argue that our actions may be sufficiently 'constrained' by our character and nature to be recognisably and identifiably ours and yet not be completely caused and determined by them, and that this constraint on them is consistent with the libertarian claim that there must be an element of unpredictability (that should be distinguished from randomness, it being inherent in the logic of true option) in our free acts.

Now discussions on this issue have been complex, but I think we can deal with it quickly for our purpose. Compatibilists like Flew, I think, assume unwarrantedly: firstly, that since our acts must issue from our nature, they must do so in such fashion as to render them amenable to predictability on a causal analysis; and secondly, that all cases of behavioural unpredictability must be chance or random behaviour. Now, since the freedom at issue in the present context of discussion is <u>human</u> freedom,* the human natures at

---

*   What we know of human freedom could then be applied analogically to our envisaged transnatural moral beings. After all, our presumption has been that these created 'spiritual' moral beings share the imperfections of humans sufficiently to choose evil, resulting, we conceive, in the spoiling of man's natural and

issue, which all responsible acts must issue from, must
be the natures we know and understand from an existential analysis of actual human beings (and not some conjectural 'perfect' natures). And from the testimonies
of, say, dramatists and novelists, we know (if there
are empirical items of knowledge at all, this must be
one of them, it being, I claim, elemental) the human
situation to be such that; firstly, even though men do
acquire more or less stable characters and dispositions, the acquiring is an on-going process that can as
the result of recalcitrant choices and actions change
directions, even though this would no doubt take place
gradually, since there would be internalised resistances of character and habits. And these resistances
would themselves be not mere causal effects but must be
explained in part at least in terms of past deliberation and choice. Secondly, even on a man's prevailing
character and dispositions, there can in principle
be no exact prediction of his choices, since there must
always exist a range of possible choices of the same
general sort he is predisposed to make. And the element of unpredictability that remains of human character development and choice, after taking stock of all
that can indeed be predicted of man's behaviour, should
not, surely, be pejoratively equated with the unpredictableness of randomness or chance. Randomness implies
unpredictableness, but this does not mean that all unpredictableness implies randomness.

Now our claim that these observations are elemental will not suffice for many, so let me add the
following demonstration and comment. Now none would,
of course, doubt the observation that we do form stable
characters that do affect our choices. If therefore I
can demonstrate that my choices could be in principle
unpredictable, I will have established my contention
that despite constraints of character and disposition,
there could still be an area of unpredictability in my
really free choices. Now I can decide now to stop
writing, have tea or otherwise, and no one would doubt
that I can effect these decisions at will. Whatever
your purported predictions as to how I would in fact
choose now, I can always falsify it if I choose to.
You say I will stop writing, and I can will to continue, and effect it. You then say I will continue, but
I can decide to stop, and do so. This can continue
indefinitely; the unpredictableness of such particular
decisions of mine is therefore a matter of principle.
We may then observe that whereas on the deterministic
and biological environments.

view of actions, our choices and acts should be in principle if not always in practice predictable, our ordinary experiences abound with such demonstrations as that given above, that show that at least some of our choices and acts can be always or in principle unpredictable. So to deny that man has free will in the sense explained and say that all his behaviour is determined would be to accept a thesis a major logical consequence of which can be in principle indefinitely falsified in quite ordinary experiences. The determinist cannot maintain his consequential 'predictability of human action' thesis, since it is demonstrable that at least some human actions are in principle unpredictable. It may be objected that the determinist need only be committed to the predictability of actions in principle, and in practice causal factors may be unknown or unknowable to him, including those that govern my successive 'intentions' to falsify his in practice imperfect attempted predictions of my actions in my demonstration. But this is double-talk. Talk of 'predictability in principle' must, to be substantive, imply at least some predictability in practice; otherwise it degenerates into an unfalsifiable dogma. And our demonstration rules out in principle any successful prediction whatever in at least some cases. It is also no use retorting that the predictability would include the predicting of my counteraction in order to falsify the initial prediction. For where will we end in this kind of talk? Suppose I answer that I can then falsify this later prediction by deciding not to proceed with the initial falsification? It could then be retorted that a full prediction could cover even this, and this talk can continue ad infinitum. Meaningful talk of predictability of actions must involve the preparedness, at least in some practical cases, to state a full prediction before the event.

Now all this shows that even though the ordinary language sense of 'morally responsible behaviour' does connote that the behaviour is the sort the agent is predisposed to doing by virtue of the character he has formed, the libertarian in the freewill-versus-determinism controversy could readily concede this and still insist that real free action, as existentially known and ordinarily understood, involves an element of unpredictability occasioned by the open-endedness of choice. True, when told that a saintly person has, say, committed rape, we ordinarily would first suspect the act to have been involuntary, since it wouldn't be recognisably his. So we would send him for psychiatric observation. But on being assured after repeated reports that he wasn't insane or the like, would and should we continue indefinitely to deny him the responsibility? Wouldn't we, and rightly, simply sigh and say something like 'alas, but the spirit is willing and the flesh is weak'? Would the plea of, say, insanity stand up in court on <u>only</u> the ground that the act was normally unpredictable of him?

The upshot of the above considerations is therefore the refutation of Flew's point <u>5</u>, for they show that it is to flout the ordinary and proper use of the term 'free acts' to conceive of God's predisposing purportedly free moral agents, by imposing constraints of character and/or other specific constraints, such that they would in each case always choose the good. Indeed, on our analysis of the innate unpredictability, within ranges of possible specific choices falling under predictable sorts of choices, of specific actual actions issuing from character and human nature, it should be in principle impossible even for almighty God to foresee the specific and actual choices of free moral agents. It would therefore be <u>in principle</u> impossible for God to provide free moral agents with the constraints of character and environment that would guarantee in advance their issuance in only good choices.* And we would have in all this a more basic refutation of the Mackie-Paluch contention discussed earlier. For as we pointed out, it is only when God is

---

* We are not here contradicting our earlier argument that God could have narrowed the range of created moral agents' possible free choices to eliminate evil or excessively evil choices without affecting their status as moral agents (Cf.pp.44-45). There, it is taken for granted that God's narrowing of the range, possibly through character and environmental constraints, <u>constitutes an infringement</u> on freedom, except that it is contended that the infringement would leave enough scope for freedom and moral agency to satisfy the minimal conditions for moral status. Now Flew's compatibility thesis precisely denies that such an interference with the possibilities of free choices would be <u>at all</u> an infringement on freedom, and asserts that even divine <u>determining</u> of all specific 'choices' would not be incompatible with our ordinary distinctions between 'free' and 'unfree' acts. It is this thesis we are here debunking, in order to uphold our theodicy based on the contention: that it is conceivable that some at least of the evil choices resulting in both what we know as moral and 'natural' evil are in principle impossible on God's part to prevent. This is for both the reasons, that the minimal range of possible choices necessary for moral freedom has to be preserved, and that

56

conceived as being capable of foreseeing the actual choices of would-be moral agents that the whole question can arise as to whether he could actualise only the subset of them who would only choose the right. Now, it is true that the claim that God has foreknowledge even of man's free choices has been made in the traditional doctrine of divine omniscience but the theist can readily concede the claim to be erroneous without necessarily revising the doctrine beyond recognition (Cf. pp. 22-23). Where a logically impossible 'feat' is concerned, God's being incapable of performance would only be due to the unintelligibility of the feat rather than show that God is any less potent, as has often enough been pointed out.

The gift of free will therefore involves a risk, even on the part of omnipotence; for it logically gives rise to the possibility of the divine will being thwarted. The only way open to God to guarantee the absence of evil choices (barring the <u>total</u> eliminating of the scope to choose the bad and leaving moral agents with the freedom to choose among degrees of good and moral neutrality - which we said could be conceived to be incompatible with the creation of moral agents) would be not to create moral beings at all. Now God willed to create moral agents, and surely the risk was worth taking. (I can't conceive of <u>human</u> beings maintaining otherwise; here again we reach the limits of our world*.) It was indeed logically possible for such created agents to actually turn out to be always choosing the good. But the created moral agents, at any rate the bad angels and mankind, <u>in fact</u> turned out to be beings many of whom have chosen and will choose the bad that lead to dire consequences. In this actuality, and in view, anyhow, of the immorality and indeed unintelligibility of the postulate of God's actualising only good beings, a loving God, omnipotence notwithstanding, can only have recourse to being the father who awaits the prodigal son to come home. He might have, and we, from the human perspective, suggested he

---

within the minimal range it is contradictory to conceive of God's guaranteeing that the actual outcomes of free choices would in each case be for good.

* Thus, any doubt cast on the worth of God's taking the said risk would itself be an exercise in free moral agency.

should have eliminated some at least of the more excessive sufferings. For it seemed to us that the other
evils left and the possibilities for neutrality and
degrees of good would be scope enough for moral agency.
Even so, the impossibility of eliminating these other
evils in the creating of the moral agents in the universe is a case suggestive enough for our theodicy.

Now if our account of free will, which is the
orthodox account of the Judaeo-Christian tradition,
seems to contradict the doctrines, within the same
tradition, of Creation and Omnipotence (a point Flew
made much of: see point 6 above), I fail to see why we
should not revise these doctrines to bring them in line
with the equally fundamental doctrine of free will.
For while the doctrines of Creation and Omnipotence can
be revised, without the loss of their identity, in such
a way as not to let them entail the ruling out of free
will, the alternative of committing the theist to
Flew's compatibilist thesis would be tantamount to drastically undermining what religion traditionally says
on the significance of man's response to God and his
quest for salvation, which depends on free will in the
sense defended above. A fair-minded account of religion, befitting philosophical enquiry, should therefore
represent it at its best, which in our present case
means we should ascribe any excessive and incompatible
claims as to the exercise of God's creative ability and
omnipotence to some believers' over-enthusiasm or to
claims made in poetic overtones, say, in adoration and
worship. Surely, if God is almighty, he could have
chosen just to create a minimal situation which will
then grow spontaneously and where created moral agents'
autonomy is preserved.

PART TWO

RELIGIOUS TRUTH-CLAIMS AND EVIDENCES

We may now proceed to examine the possibility
of having positive grounds for religious truth-claims,
having in the foregoing provided sufficient arguments,
I think, to enable the suspension of our disbelief in
religion despite its apparent conceptual incoherences.
Our conclusion on the issue of conceptual incoherences
depends importantly, we said, on the outcome of the
discussion we will now begin, since the suspension of
disbelief recommended is in anticipation of our having
independent grounds for belief. Now the problem of
evil can be seen not only as threatening the internal
coherence of religion but also as being counter-evidence to its truth-claims. But obviously our arguments
about the problem in Part One also suffice to enable us
to allay our scepticism on this score, pending the outcome of the following discussion.

I shall show that a potentially fertile avenue
for the ascertaining of theistic truth-claims exists
in the consideration of purported miracles; which in
some conceivable contexts, in conjunction with certain
other factors, could render it reasonable to believe
in theism. We shall discuss this in the context of a
quick rejection, if taken by themselves, of some recent
renewed attempts to bolster theism on the usual traditional grounds. These attempts are representations of
those in recent philosophical theology which have either
disclaimed the importance of allegedly supernatural
phenomena like miracles and special religious experiences, or have in the process provided reductivist
accounts of them. Improvements on the traditional arguments they purportedly are and they are claimed to
have circumvented the usual objections to their traditional counterparts. I shall show that they face the
usual objections, and in this way illustrate that without the crucial support of an argument from miracles
and special religious experiences, such grounds for
theism will, as a matter of logic, remain arbitrary
from the viewpoint of public rationality, however ingen-
iously improved they may be on the traditional proofs.
I shall then show that a case built upon claims to
miracles has the potential to salvage some such grounds

by giving them the warrant they in themselves lack. Also, although by themselves they would not be significant enough for our purpose, we shall see that they are not totally devoid of evidential value, and some of them could serve to suggest possible directions for authenticated further testings of a more personal nature of religious truth-claims once their evidential value had been reinforced in collaboration with ascertained miracles. Generally, the traditional theistic 'proofs', with whatever insufficient evidential value they provide, considered in the light of the possibility of ascertaining miracles, should be sufficient at least to put the religious explanations of the universe as a serious hypothesis to truth, deserving of attention as such in the liberal education curriculum. I shall however suggest that my 'miracles-based' theistic case will also be the warrant for the analogous testings of 'miracles' and 'religious experiences' of a less public and more personal nature in the context of an individual's own life. It may be - and this is quite in line with the usual claim that religious commitment is in the end a personal decision to be made by the individual alone - that the purported realm of religious truths is unique in, among other things, the fact that, although a believer should indeed have been initiated into religious enquiry via in part a consideration of public evidences, in the end commitment must, in the logic of the matter, be not a matter of having publicly attested proofs. For we have indicated with John Hick (Cf. p. 38) that an epistemic distance might have to be maintained between man and God if free response to God were to be in practice psychologically possible. And in suggesting this, we are not advocating blind faith, which would not be much of a choice in religious response. For we think that reasons, initially publicly attested ones, and eventually and crucially more personal ones, analogous to the public ones but lacking in public compellingness, which are convincing only to initiates who have begun already the search for truth ('Seek and ye shall find. Knock and it shall be opened unto you'), have a place in the 'leap' into conviction and religious awareness.

In thus arguing for a crucial role for miracles in religious apologetics, I am of course not also claiming that this is the only way to rational belief. Other objective-enough grounds cannot be ruled out to rescue the traditional purported theistic grounds from over-esoterism. I am only concerned with arguing one case, which would be minimally sufficient for mooting religion as an interesting and serious hypothesis to a distinct realm of truth, deserving of attention in the liberal curriculum. However, the success of my contention will mean a sort of restoration of purported miracles to their traditionally key position in Christian apologetics.

I SOME RECENTLY PURPORTED GROUNDS

First, let us see how the recent attempts to revive the traditional theistic proofs fail just like the latter when taken by themselves.

The criticisms of the traditional proofs amount to saying that any attempt to impose a design-pattern on cosmic features which would purportedly intimate divine presence but which could well be interpreted secularistically, and any attempt to give religious significance to what could be quite ordinary experiences, would be tantamount to imposing an arbitrary interpretation on things. This then cannot be a ground for God's existence, fundamentally because it is precisely theistic presumptions that have produced it. And it is no use retorting that all seeing or experiencing is interpretive -- seeing-as or experiencing-as (see Hick, 1969). For even after granting the point, a distinction still persists between well-grounded, inescapable and undisputed interpretations, and those like the theistic postulate, which are arbitrary, and result only from prior belief. Thus, whereas our seeing a machine before us as a motor-car would enable us to infer that the manufacturer exists, this would not hold for our seeing a moving cloud as a racing car.*

One attempt to base theism mainly on an examination of cosmic features is that of A. Boyce Gibson (Gibson, 1970). He claims that in 'looking for those features of the world that have the greatest persistence and constancy' he is 'looking' and 'not inventing

---

* Kai Nielsen has argued against Hick that seeing is sensibly 'seeing-as' only where there is also such a thing as squarely seeing (Nielsen, 1971, p. 86). Putting it this way against Hick is question-begging, for Hick is saying that even such supposed seeings are really seeing-as. And it has to be conceded that some tutoring is necessary before seeings can take place.

or asking what we are contributing to the interpretation of things' (p. 63). He identifies what he calls
'the drift to order' and 'the drift to creativity' in
the 'structures' of the cosmos, and maintains that they
'are discerned as unfinished but demanding fulfilment'
so that 'we can best make sense of them if we see in
them the continuation . . . of a divine presence.' The
incompletion, which is also present in human experience, is 'the consequence of an unfinished universe'
and it points 'beyond the horizon'. 'Both order and
creation are most efficacious . . . when they exceed
their own average . . . if they hold the ultimate
reserve power over chaos and torpor', and 'their un-
restricted operation points back to the unrestricted-
ness of their source' (pp. 75-77). Note that it is
the features of the cosmos that we purportedly see by
just 'looking', and 'religious experience' which 'is
not a separate compartment of life' that are appealed
to. And Gibson proffers a reductionistic account of
miracles (pp. 267-270).

Now, theological presumptions are obvious in
Gibson's use of the words 'fulfilment', 'incompletion'
and 'creativity', and the interpretive notion of a
'drift' to either order or creativity. Clearly, presuppositions as regards what would constitute completion and fulfilment had first to be made before it
makes sense to talk of incompletion and unfulfilment.
Why shouldn't the cosmic features and human experience
as we find them be accepted as they are, and, if we
like, regarded as complete? At any rate, might not the
'incompletion' be interpreted as neutralising the
claims made for order and creativity, rather than treated as a separate facet that calls for completion when
judged against the purportedly creativity-order facet?

The arbitrariness of Gibson's account is most
apparent in his attempt to shelve the 'counter-instance'
(i.e. innocent suffering) to his thesis away from 'the
context of contemplation'. He would only account for
evil within the context of personal faith and commitment - 'in the context of a particular revelation, we
see how the promise (of deliverance) might be fulfill-
ed'. He observes that 'if everyone took his suffering
sacrificially, spinning radiance out of it . . . it
would at least serve as a beacon to other sufferers,
and if the impact were strong enough it might take them
out of their suffering altogether' (pp. 198-9).

Now, fundamentally, Gibson cannot evade the problem of evil at the level of contemplation precisely because it is an objection that strikes at that level. If he can't accommodate evil there, then he would not have his initial account of 'order and creativity' with which to warrant our suspension of judgement till we see how the problem is met in particular situations of personal faith and commitment. In any case, even if suffering could be transformed to joy in the personal context, this would only bring credit to the sufferer rather than vindicate the situation God is supposed to have 'ordered'. The 'consecration of suffering' (p. 202) cannot eliminate suffering, for the consecration can take place only after suffering is experienced. It is also interesting to ask why, if to Gibson the incompletion of the cosmos points beyond to God, evil is not regarded as another feature, or the result, of incompletion. Another Christian philosopher might develop the case along this line, the possibility of which only confirms our point that Gibson had not looked at the world and then found God intimated in its features, but had rather presumed theism and then sought to see the cosmos and the human situation as theism would have him see.

Other efforts via observing cosmic features take the form of reappraising the traditional design and cosmological arguments. Assertions are that these arguments should rather be viewed as clarificatory of the consistency, vis-a-vis the cosmic features, of the theistic world-view, or that they serve only to confirm theists in their belief by showing the sort of consistency; or that, although they provide no compelling reason for belief, together they effect a cosmic disclosure and enable an extra-rational 'leap of faith'. (Traces of the sort of reappraisal are found in Gibson, 1970; Lewis, 1959; Owens, 1969; Hick, 1970). It cannot be denied that these attempts are meant to provide some reasons for theism, for it is implied that the consistency referred to argues for theism, or that showing that this is the sort of world God could have made would lend credence to theism, or that the cosmic disclosure isn't too unreasonably effected. Now, Gibson's case is enough to show that the mere tallying of cosmic features with the religious worldview is insufficient to support the latter. And since theism comes prior to such efforts at seeing-the-world-as, any leap of faith, rather than mediated by the efforts, would have occurred prior to the whole endeavour.

Attempts based on purported religious experience are exemplified in the work of H.D. Lewis and William James (Lewis, 1959; James 1941). To Lewis, religious experience begins with an 'initial insight into . . . some complete and unconditioned source . . . of realities . . . '. 'It is one apprehension, one leap of thought' by which understanding 'the meaning of . . . the mysterious source' means also appreciating 'the inevitability by which (the source) must be so'. This 'elusive insight . . . has the same compelling character as . . . logic and mathematics' (Chapt. 2). We find ourselves 'startled into sobering and perhaps terrifying realisation of the limitations of (our) own existence and activity and their involving a source beyond themselves' which is 'overwhelmingly mysterious . . . unlimited or absolute being'. With this initial insight will come 'a heightening of perceptiveness . . . directed mainly to matters most consonant with . . . the new perspective into which all things are cast when viewed in the light of our altered notions of their boundaries' (Chap. 5). Events and lives permeated by the religious awareness will thus have recognisable 'patterns of experience' which are further evidence of the deity. But Lewis insists that religious experience is not 'the intrusion of a wholly unusual factor into the normal occasions of life, or something peculiar'. Rather 'it will not be possible to note and record precisely the part which distinctive religious experiences play in our lives, or to determine exactly when they arise and fade again into others'. Yet he says that 'we are able to recognise, in a general way, and in our life as a whole', the impact and meaning of the experiences.*

Now, Lewis' religious insight really comprises an unwarranted inference from data. It is one thing to be 'startled' by a sense of finiteness, and quite another to conclude that this intimates the existence

---

* H.P. Owens (Op. Cit.) shares similar views. Even if we view their work as descriptive analysis the apologetic intentions are implicit if we remember that at the level of essentially contested analysis there can be no neutrality (See Tan, 1978, pp. 34-44; Gallie, 1964, Chap. 8) and that if they succeed in delineating certain experiences to be uniquely religious, theism would already be a foregone conclusion in the analysis.

of 'absolute being', however psychologically disinclined one was at such profound moments to sort them out. Indeed the former could well be a common datum of mortal experience, but whether one should as a result despair, or see God, or merely accept a brute fact, is precisely the point. Thus, it cannot be that the insight has the compelling character of logic, and it is dubious whether Lewis really means that, for he also admits that 'not all have this insight; it is not psychologically necessary'. But then what could he mean by the comparison with logic if not to say that only those already religiously initiated would feel the compulsion? This however merely shows that theism has been presumed, a factor which also shows in Lewis' claim that understanding 'the meaning' of God would involve appreciating that he must be so. For only the emotionally committed would find it as a matter of fact hard to separate understanding the notion 'God' from praising and adoring God. As such, Lewis' assertion, that the insight would usher the initiate into an extra-dimensional perception of natural phenomena, so that religiously meaningful patterns previously unseen are now detected, merely illustrates again the sort of arbitrariness we saw in Gibson's case. As regards the view that religious experience is not something wholly unusual or precisely identifiable, we ask how then might we recognise, generally or otherwise, the experience and its import. It is true that 'we murder to dissect' in some contexts, but in the case of a general impression as controversial as the impact of 'religious experience', dissection in the form of particularly determining what constitutes the experience and distinguishes it from other experiences is essential in-sofar as this is the only way to begin independently to test the claim. Moreover, any factor that really calls for anything like a religious explanation must be strikingly different from the usual. And Lewis' claim, that 'the moments of religious insight are sharper' on occasions like those 'of grave and outstanding need', fares no better; for convincing, indeed proven, naturalistic explanations already exist for such psychic states. Lewis' case seems therefore an attempt to retain the general impression even after the particulars which give it steam have been watered away.

William James aims to 'offer something that may fit the facts so easily that your scientific logic will find no plausible pretext for vetoing your impulse to welcome it as true' (p. 511). However, all he claims is that there is an analogous scientific postulate, i.e.

'the subconscious', which might be 'the mediating term' for 'the more of religion' (i.e. more than 'the material world all over again'). 'The more', on its 'hither side', may be viewed as 'the subconscious continuation of our conscious life' (p. 152). But, surely, this is only to say that what theists regard as religious experience already has a naturalistic explanation, and nothing is asserted which could distinguish religious experience from normal experience; in fact the thesis unwittingly affirms that 'religious' experience need not be religious at all. Thus the case rather subtracts credibility from 'the further side' of religion. Indeed, James' account is reductionistic of his religious 'over-beliefs'. The contention that the religious man is moved by an external power is, to James, only 'vindicated' by the scientific observation that 'it is one of the peculiarities of invasions from the subconscious region to take on objective appearances and to suggest to the subject an external control' (pp. 512-3). And his religious 'over-beliefs' and 'God' are explained thus:

> 'The further limits of our being plunge into an altogether other dimension of existence from the sensible and merely "understandable" world . . . so long as our ideal impulses originate in this region . . . we belong to it in a more intimate sense than that in which we belong to the visible world, for we belong in the most intimate sense wherever our ideals belong - yet this unseen region in question is not merely ideal, for it produces effects in this world . . . that which produces effects within another reality must be termed a reality itself . . . so I will call this higher part of the universe by the name of God (p. 516).

If this is all James means by 'reality' and 'God', then perhaps he has provided theism with an empirical base, though only in the fashion of Braithwaite's empiricist reductionistic view of religious beliefs (Braithwaite, 1971; see also our Introduction, pp. x-xi). Generally, James has got his sequence of proof wrong. Explanations other than the established scientific ones are called for only after the latter prove inadequate. James in effect has only shown that scientific explanations are already adequate for the phenomena dubbed 'religious experiences'. The reason for this curious confusion, I think, is again the arbitrary presumption of theism. Given that religious experiences are really experiences of God, then showing that such experiences, considered scientifically, could have occurred (and occurred commonly for that matter, since there is even a scientific terminology for the sort of experience) would of course further the apologetic cause.

It might be objected that such apologetic attempts, despite their appearance, do not draw conclusions from data. Seeing God as being intimated in cosmic features and human experience is one whole apprehension in itself, empirically reputable as a unit of experience. Now, we noted Lewis' description of religious insight as 'one leap of thought'. (Lewis says of the traditional theistic proofs that 'where the arguments fail is in trying to break into a series of steps what is in fact one insight' (p. 43)). Owens and Gibson too believe in some sort of basic, irreducible intuition into religious truth. But then when they proceed in their books to systematise the findings of their 'basic apprehension' of things, inferences are made and conclusions drawn, if not explicitly, then implicitly, in ways we have made explicit. This is necessarily so, for God could not be a factor for direct encounter, so that any 'apprehension' of him in the nature of things must be inferential. (The word 'mediated' is preferred, but what else can it mean than that certain phenomena had facilitated the inference that God exists?) But this is where the usual objections to natural theology apply. The whole attempt is really the same thing in another guise, a manoeuvre that further suggests that theism has been presumed.

Could it be claimed in defence, in this context, that religious grounds are unique and we have erred in weighing them by the usual criteria? Thus, Lewis contends that theistic statements are supportable only by the appropriate evidence (pp. 20-34) which is in intuition and experience (although he thinks the intuition is universal if only all who have it would recognise it). Owens agrees with Lewis, although he describes the intuition in a way that (tellingly) renders it no more unique: 'an insight that is mediated by finite data and that is achieved through the normal powers of the mind'.* Owens himself had made claims

---

*   See Religious Studies, Vol. 7, p. 175.

such as that 'when a believer is asked "why do you believe in God?", he can give two answers: "because I apprehend God and because my belief satisfies all the relevant rational criteria"' (Owens, 1969, p. 176). The 'apprehension' of God is one irreducible uniquely religious datum, and the 'rational criteria' are exclusively the religiously relevant ones. Hick also suggests that 'a sufficiently vivid religious experience would entitle a man to claim to know that God is real' for 'in his own experience of the presence of God he has a good and compelling reason to be sure of it'. (Hick, 1967, p. 210).

Much has been said in criticism of such esoteric claims to uniqueness; so I shall merely observe that they rest on a false analogy drawn between the purported unique religious experience and the distinctiveness of the various secular forms of truth. Even if we concede that the forms of truth enquiry were so distinct from each other as to admit of no similarity at all in the ways evidence is construed (which is clearly false), there is still a sense of their being open to public scrutiny which does not obtain in the purported 'uniqueness' of religious experience. A sufficiently liberal education might make the secular truth-discourses intelligible in some respects to some, and the invitation is always open to all to be initiated sufficiently into the disciplines in order to test the evidences occurring therein. At any rate, we rest assured in that many from among us, whose initial qualification for the enterprise had only been in having the common sense we are all endowed with to some degree, had been initiated into the respective disciplines, and we accept their expert opinions. In the case of the purported religious experience, however, it is precisely that unique 'evidences' are claimed to be unrecognisable to the uninitiated, and that the initiation necessary is claimed to require, as an initial qualification, such non-universally available, extra-rational or quasi-rational impulses like 'a leap of thought' or some 'elusive insight' that cause the analogy between the claims to uniqueness to break down. It can of course always be claimed that all who submit themselves sufficiently would recognise the 'insight'. But this remains only a claim, and made only by those already initiated. (It is precisely because such esoterism of evidence is unacceptable as a claim to truth that we aim to show, especially in the following sections of this part, the possibility of having public grounds to reinforce the more personal truth-claims of religion, and thus moot religion to be a respectable claim to distinct and transcendent knowledge over and above the secular forms of knowledge.)

Finally, Gibson argues at some length that the assumption that theism is essentially far removed from empiricism is a 'misadventure'. However, we will see that it is his own understanding of the empiricist challenge (Op. Cit. Chapter 1) that is a misadventure. All he says to make the point is that sense-data are abstractions, and that awareness is really 'of things-in-relation', 'continuous', 'intentional', 'object-discovering' and is 'inescapable from valuations' (pp. 26, 27). But we have indicated before that on conceding the point, what follows is only that the way we look at phenomena is essentially interpretive, so that the theistic view is at best a contestant inter-pretation among viewings-as. If theism were purported-ly 'empirical' only in this sense, then the empiricist objector could readily concede the point, although further considerations, as we noted, would be needed to decide if it was a plausible seeing-as. The theistic world-view would only be, to borrow a phrase from William James, 'the materialistic world over again', although it is precisely when new theistic facts are postulated to explain the phenomena that theism becomes interesting, but also problematic in the face of the verificationist challenge. It is not an interpretation per se that is under the verificationist onslaught but the postulate of a 'spiritual' order of reality where personages and God exist. The question then is how we could, in the style of the true empiricist, infer from the observable world the existence of such 'spiritual facts'. The postulate of 'spiritual' personages, while it might be warranted by a convincing interpretation of phenomena, can never be part of the interpretation it-self. The question then is, if spiritual beings by definition cannot be empirically known, whether the theistic world view could ever warrant the postulate. The best interpretation of phenomena would not consti-tute an empirical encounter with the deity.

T.R. Miles, whose reductionistic view of reli-gion we noted before (Cf. p.xi) has accused theists of committing an unwarranted linguistic 'shift' of meaning by construing the God of religious experience as a non-material being existing like the 'man-in-the-top-flat'. He calls this 'the absolute-existence mistake' and opines that if the theist 'is to claim that a non-mat-erial Being exists, he must be prepared to say what

69

difference the existence of such a Being would make, or perhaps better, what is achieved by the language which asserts his existence . . .' (Miles, 1972, pp.29-31). Now, this is a pertinent objection to the apologetic attempts we have been considering. Providing theism with natural grounds means, when no theistic assumptions are made, applying the positivistic criteria even to the core of religious beliefs, i.e. the postulate of God. And since 'God' cannot be empirically tested, and since from natural phenomena nothing besides arbitrary theistic interpretations may conceivably be postulated, any affirmation that God exists, purportedly based on purely natural grounds, can only be figurative. If literalness is claimed, then indeed an unwarranted linguistic shift of meaning would be committed, for, strictly on natural grounds, the only sense that our language can encase must be subjected to the usual criteria of meaningfulness.

II   THE CONCEIVABILITY AND POSSIBILITY OF THEISTIC
      EVIDENCES

        Our above discussions show that whatever evidential value purported grounds for religion of the sort sampled may have, they fail by themselves to significantly affirm religious truth-claims. I shall now suggest that they are not entirely devoid of evidential value, and argue that such value as they have, combined crucially with possible evidences from considering claims to miracles and, as a corollary, special experiences, could provide at least the initial affirmative grounds we need to moot religion as a viable claim to truth.

        Now I think that purported grounds for theism of the sort discussed above succeed in showing that human experience, cosmic features, or other phenomena are amenable to being viewed as the outcome of divine purpose and creation, and they therefore already constitute some evidence for religion, even though by themselves they are insufficiently significant for our case for religion. For had the cosmos not existed or had it not the features that would render the postulate of a cosmic designer conceivable, or were human experience and the pattern of human life such that they could never be conceivably interpreted as having the religious import Lewis, Gibson and others want to give them (however arbitrary such conceptions are from the viewpoint of giving hard evidences), then the question of

70

divine orderliness and creation or cosmic purpose could not even arise. There would not then exist the entire framework within which the theistic postulate is at least intelligible, if not rationally compelling. So the experiential and cosmic features appealed to in such apologies for religion do have the evidential value for establishing the religious explanation of things as conceivably one among other intelligible explanatory possibilities. The significant counter experiential feature is suffering which Gibson, we saw, hasn't successfully treated. But we have already argued, in Part One, for its possible accommodation within a purposive and good creation.

However, the mere conceivability and possibility of a religious explanation of things are insufficient to establish it as a contender to truth deserving of serious consideration. In the elimination of explanatory postulates and contentions judged to be unworthy of consideration (as required by Occam's razor and from the standpoint of public rationality), unless some initial evidences, or at least the conceivability and practical possibility of having such evidences, exist to raise a particular postulate above the level of mere speculative intelligibility, where other equally intelligible postulates are possible, it should rightly be put aside. (Where a postulate is the only conceivable explanation where an explanation is called for, then it of course deserves greater respect, even though this has to be provisional, since we could be wrong about the inconceivability of other explanations.) It may be said that mere 'conceivability and practical possibility of having such evidences' is still insufficient. But I think this refusal would be unduly exclusive. Where an explanatory conjecture is 'concretised' to such a level as the laying down of the exact procedures for its testing, and where the latter are independently judged to be appropriate and adequate, I think rationality demands that we try it out before rejecting it. The alternative of ruling it out at the start is rational only where there seems no way it can be tested in any case. Further, just as the mere intelligibility of an explanatory postulate has in itself some, though insufficient, evidential value, so the additional presence of verification procedures for it would mean this much additional evidential value for it. For if it were true, there must indeed be some aspects of our experience or the world that would somewhat tally with it and it would therefore be testable in terms of those aspects. Testability, therefore, is an additional indication of truth. However, I have already said that, in our following discussion of the crucial place of miracles and special experiences in religious apologetics, I shall indicate areas where we may claim to have more than the evidential value of mere testability, especially the area of our personal lives. All this would I think suffice to place the religious explanation of things among the theories worthwhile considering and teaching from the standpoint of public rationality, even though it may already suffice for a reasonable personal leap of thought and faith possibly permitted by the distinctive and internal logic of religious truth enquiry. Be it remembered that if religion is true, then the distinctness of religious discourse must necessarily be something quite distinct from the sort of logical differences between the secular discourses. It could well be that this warrants a greater degree of esoterism in the validating of religious truth-claims than that permitted by the canons of ordinary public rationality. Thus, it may be that the crux of the issue, in the rational believer's personal life-experience, is whether or not there exist, albeit judged from a more or less esoteric perspective, religiously significant and 'miraculous' events, whose intelligibility and creditability are supported by the case to be argued for the public intelligibility of miracles and of evidences for them, and which will suffice to tip the balance of contestant explanatory possibilities of the universe hovering above the pre-believing mind in favour of religion, and thus facilitate a rational leap of faith. The balance of explanatory possibilities is of course maintained by those explanatory hypotheses of the universe which, like what we said of the religious hypothesis, pass the initial test of intelligibility. Although we said that more is required than mere intelligibility to render such hypotheses worthy of consideration as judged by public rationality, in the area of personal rational belief which the peculiar logic of religion may well warrant, the mere intelligibility of the religious view might already be profoundly significant. Now all these indications of the possibility of a rational confirmation of theism in one's personal life-experience should also bolster our contention for the deservingness of the religious explanatory hypothesis from the standpoint of public rationality, since, as we have said, where an avenue exists for testing a hypothesis, it would be unduly high-handed not to entertain it. And in the case of the religious hypothesis, traditions of believers in

72

diverse cultures, including numerous who in other respects are acknowledged as outstanding thinkers, have testified to such personal confirmations of their beliefs.

(i) The Intelligibility of Miracles and the Possibility of their Confirmation

Before discussing the crucial place of miracles (and, in that context, of special events in our case for religion), we have to argue for their conceptual viability and the practical possibility of ascertaining claims to miracles. For Hume, and in our time notably Antony Flew interpreting Hume, have denied miracles on these counts. Other contemporary writers have tried to answer Flew but have misunderstood him and confused the issue. The best way to clarify Flew's views is therefore via an examination and sorting out of these confusions. As this issue is crucial to our defence of religion, dwelling on it in this way will anyhow be worthwhile. I shall eventually rebut the Humean theses.

By miracles, we of course mean at least purported violations, by supernatural agency, of natural laws. For any account of miracles that reduces them to merely attempts to ascribe a religious significance to what could well be ordinary unsurprising natural events would place claims to miracles along with the sorts of traditional arguments for religion we have shown above to be not evidentially significant enough for us. On the other hand, if miracles on the 'violation' model were ascertained, then, as will be elaborated, explanation in terms of the supernatural would be compelled.

Flew has opined (1) that the logic of descriptive natural laws renders miracles, on the violation-model, in principle unidentifiable; and (2) that in the absence of a natural theology or an authentic revelation that could identify a miraculous occurrence, the methodology of critical history would preclude as genuinely historical any evidence that could indicate a miraculous occurrence (Flew, 1966, Chap. 7; Flew, 1967). I shall discuss and answer these objections in turn.

The first objection is that the conceptual difficulty in the definition of miracles as events overriding natural laws gives rise to the 'problem of identifying an event as miraculous' (Flew, 1967, p.348);

for the scientist has no criterion to distinguish between falsifications of established laws and 'overridings' of them. Ascertaining a particular occurrence to be a miracle requires one 'to prove simultaneously both the rule and the exception, but still without "a mutual destruction of arguments"'. (Flew, 1961, p. 202). A writer, R.C. Wallace,has replied that a claim to the miraculous is 'rather that with reference to one and the same law, it is true both that it seems to be applicable in a situation, and yet that it is shown not to be so by the subsequent course of events' (Wallace, 1970, p. 238). But this is evasive. Flew is not saying that claims to miracles involve 'asserting that with reference to one and the same occurrence a given law both does and does not apply', but that once we have the exception we do not have the rule, whereas claims to miracles need both the rule and the exception. 'The subsequent course of events' would invalidate the law, for the scientist insists 'on always seeking strictly universal laws' (Flew, 1967, p. 349). Wallace thinks that Flew's charge 'could be brought only if the exception were merely apparent and in time could be assimilated within a suitably revised law', but he observes that claims to miracles have a 'different status' and that a miracle 'does not remain as an exception of the kind that science can and must investigate'. But Flew would say that we are logically committed to regard proven exceptions as 'apparent' and 'if a (miraculous) occurrence is to serve as an endorsement of some doctrinal system, the method of identification must be logically independent of that system' (Ibid p. 348). The issue is not'what is thinkable and what is not' (Wallace, Ibid), but what can conceivably be independently identified.

Ninian Smart, in answer to Flew, distinguishes between repeatable counter-instances to natural laws and non-repeatable counter-instances, and understands violations of natural laws as non-repeatable counter-instances (Smart, 1964, Chap. 2). This is on the right track, for some independent criteria could be proffered to indicate the extent to which counter-instances can be taken as non-repeatable. R.G. Swinburne, discussing such criteria, opines that a counter-instance may be assumed to be non-repeatable, not only when no new formula can be constructed which yields more successful predictions, nor one fairly simple relative to the data, but also when 'data continue to accumulate' which show the established formula to be 'a completely successful predictor' (Swinburne, 1968, p. 322; 1970, pp. 29-32).

Swinburne suggests the view, also suggested by R.F. Holland (whose views we will presently mention) and Wallace, that a violation of a natural law can be understood in terms of an ascertained occurrence, the non-repeatability of which has been and is being confirmed by data in such abundance that the 'evidence' indicates that withholding a decision on the matter pending future discoveries becomes academic. Explaining his 'violation concept of the miraculous' in terms necessarily, though not sufficiently, of a 'conflict of certainties', Holland illustrates his point with the miracle of Jesus turning water into wine and concludes that the presence of a natural cause of the alleged phenomenon is conceptually impossible (Holland, 1967, p. 168). This 'certainty' rests on available data on the conditions under which wine is obtained. When it conflicts with an 'empirically certain' occurrence of the phenomenon, we have an occurrence of the violation concept of miracles. Also, Wallace's thesis, that to persist in search for a scientific explanation of the resurrection 'would cast an unnecessary doubt on our standard assumptions about the uniformity of nature, and not only on our formulations of the particular laws in which that uniformity consists' (Op. Cit. p. 241), rests on abundant confirmations that a decaying corpse doesn't rise back to life.

But this defence, as it stands, is unable to cope with Flew's answer that it is incoherent for advocates of miracles, 'in the face of something which actually happens', to 'still insist that here we have an example of something which nature left to her own devices could never manage' (Flew, 1961, p. 203). Suppose we have 'empirical certainty' that an ordinary man, with no ideological association, who died of a common ailment, has arisen back to life while awaiting burial. Wouldn't conferences be immediately convened to study perhaps the literal possibility for future men of a new lease of life? On failing to explain this, wouldn't we be at a loss to do otherwise than to record it as a natural wonder to remain a challenge to researchers? The assumption that the occurrence, considered singly, was natural, though as yet unexplainable, would not go against the grain of overwhelming evidence. The evidence points to a regularity which manifests itself in all standard situations. What is assumed need only be that there is a natural exception to the regularity. Now such an exception, if scientifically explained, would then appear repeatable, though it might not in fact ever be repeated, since the conditions necessary for this might never recur. If not explained (it might even be as inconceivably explainable as the process of water turning into wine), then we can only say that, according to our present knowledge, we cannot detail the conditions for the phenomenon repeating.

Even if it could be concluded that an exception is not repeatable, the occurrence could never substantiate the violation concept of miracles. This issues from Flew's point 'that it is a contingent, if important matter of fact that the universe is as uniform we find it to be' (cited by Wallace, Op. Cit. p. 240). Wallace claims that an implication of this is that 'conceivably the universe, or particular parts of it might not be uniform', and that this provides for the emergence of 'an intelligible concept of miracles in terms of an "uncaused event"'. But if nature is only contingently uniform, then there could conceivably be natural lapses in uniformity. This means that even if an exceptional occurrence can be shown to be non-repeatable, it could still be taken as just a natural lapse in uniformity and therefore in principle unexplainable in terms of repeated occurrences of the same phenomenon. 'Uncaused' in this sense perhaps, but it cannot by itself warrant the conclusion that nature is overridden.

I think, however, that Flew's position can be shown to be unduly sceptical if miracles are considered in connection with their religious context. Suppose we have empirical certainty that an exceptional phenomenon, which to the best of our knowledge it is inconceivable that it is repeatable (or is repeatable but only in very rare circumstances), has occurred in connexion with an ideological personality, the exceptionality of the occurrence being relevant in supporting his ideology. Assume, say, that Jesus had really predicted his own death and resurrection, claimed his miraculous feats to be deliberate so as to demonstrate his 'Sonship' to the 'Father', and that we have empirical certainty that there were a few occasions at least where such exceptional phenomena occurred in strict coincidence with such demonstrations of his divinity. Now, one such occurrence, although enough to generate wonder, might be reasonably presumed after deliberation to be an accidentally coinciding natural phenomenon. Such a conclusion, though, would already seem unduly sceptical if, say, the raising of Lazarus was the only miracle of Jesus. For Jesus had confidently ordered the removal of the grave stone, prayed aloud that God should there prove his power, and then cried 'Lazarus, come forth!' And he did. And if such feats had indeed been so frequent as to be common in the life of such a person, then even if it be conceded that the exceptions, though unrepeatable or rarely repeatable, are nevertheless merely natural phenomena, the question still left unanswered is why the repeated coincidence of such rarity within the intentions and performances of this one man obtains. And what if this is only one of numerous other such men within the religious tradition? Can we conceive of an ordinary, natural regularity, that relates such exceptional events with the intentions and commands of a sort of religious personage? At some such point, abandoning scepticism would be more rational, because here some of our ordinary criteria (which are independent of religious considerations), governing the rational acceptability of purported coincidences as merely ordinary natural ones, would not be met. Here is where some criteria (those enabling us to treat the occurrence as an ordinary natural phenomenon) clash with some other criteria (those governing our treating it as purely coincidental). Flew's criticism would now be irrelevant, for our point is that an exceptional occurrence can only be rationally explained in terms of supernatural intervention, whether or not nature left to her own devices could manage it. Be it also noted that our way of identifying miracles would of course answer in the affirmative the further question as to whether such exceptional occurrences can be ascribed to the agency of a god.

The concept of miracles implicit in my position would require only Holland's 'contingency' concept in terms of a naturally explainable, albeit religiously significant, event occurring coincidentally, for example, with a woman's prayer for it to happen (Op. Cit. pp. 155-7). Though the occurrence 'cannot without confusion be taken as a sign of divine interference with the natural order' (Ibid), it can in the right context render rational the ascription of its cause to supernatural intervention (intervening, albeit, via natural means) when, as exemplified above, it is, if repeatable, only rarely so. This means that only this strong sense of the contingency concept can render claims to the miraculous interesting, a point which Holland might note. However, miracles on this concept would still be modelled on the violation-of-nature conception, since, despite their happening via natural means, they would not have occurred without divine overriding of what in fact the spontaneous natural course of events would have been.

We now face the second objection, i.e. that there could never be acceptable historical evidence to support belief in miracles. Wallace mistakes Flew to 'be mounting objections against testimony for the miraculous solely on the . . . inherent weakness of historical as opposed to scientific evidence', and insists that since Flew contrasts historical explanations against scientific ones, he cannot claim the historical to be defective solely on their being distinct. (Op. Cit. p. 233) Flew's thesis is rather that the critical historian, in his assessment of a 'candidate historical proposition' to decide if it can 'be interpreted as historical evidence at all' (Flew, 1967, p. 351),has to use as criteria the probabilities and possibilities which science has established. It is not science being opposed to history, but history having to utilise the findings of science. The position would be discrediting much else besides (Wallace, Op. Cit.p.233), but Flew has rightly pointed out that the critical historian has no choice in this, and that if he ever changes his mind, he would have done so precisely through employing the same method, applied in the light of relevant improvements to scientific knowledge. **Flew,** though, is guilty of a misjudgement, which renders plausible Wallace's view that the position 'would render er scientific theory . . . too immune to counter-evidence and subsequent change'. (Op. Cit. p. 237) Flew points to the pastness (and therefore untestability) of candidate historical propositions to contrast them unfavourably with established nomologicals. (Flew, 1967, p. 352. Now, an occurrence of <u>any unexpected</u> recalcitrance could, when first detected, be only expressible in the past tense and would usually be in the first instance singular and particular. Flew should have drawn the contrast in terms of the <u>repeatability</u> of purported occurrences. One way in which nomologicals are modified is by repeating, experimentally, noted irregularities. However singular, particular or long past the initially noted irregularity may be, it could effect a modification of nomologicals only if it is experimentally repeatable. This could still rule out natural but rare recalcitrances, but the scientific quest being to decide only after establishing high probabilities, the scientific mind has to remain sceptical after failing to repeat or explain them.

The position would not deny 'apparently anomalous facts' '<u>bona fide</u> status as actual facts',

(Wallace, Op. Cit. p. 237), but would only so treat anomalies that are unrepeatable and unexplainable, even if only as yet. Nor would Flew's position 'beg the question' (Wallace, Op. Cit. p. 234) for though 'miracles would be occasional . . . not supported by the kind of evidence the scientist can cite' (Ibid), it is precisely after the believer has maintained the apologetic role of miracles that it is contended defensively that to play the role, 'the method of (their) identification must be logically independent of that system' (Flew, 1967, p. 349).

But shouldn't the critical historian not as yet rule out purported evidences of improbable occurrences as non-genuine, but first test for the repeatability of the occurences? However, qua historian, he can only accept the body of scientific knowledge as given. And performing such tests being the scientist's job, there is every chance for the historian to reassess the evidences in the light of new scientific information. Miracles, though, are by definition unrepeatable experimentally.

Swinburne also hasn't fully taken this point of Flew's. He answers (1) that historical evidences can be just as numerous as scientific evidences (Swinburne, 1968, pp. 323-325; 1970, pp. 42-47); and (2) that historical evidences are established in largely the same way as scientific laws; and therefore, where they conflict with the laws, they should be taken as more or less probable depending on whether their probability is more or less established than that of the laws. (Swinburne, 1970, pp. 43-47) Flew would answer that since evidences can't be established independently of science, a conflict between the two cannot occur. If evidences are numerous and 'established as reliable by well-established correlations' (Swinburne, Op. Cit. p. 43) they are so precisely because, in each case, the 'correlations' are 'well-established' only if they tally with science.

Flew's position is strong against views, like Swinburne's (also Holland's 'we should upgrade . . . the probability attaching to particular events and states of affairs, so as to allow that some, as opposed to others, can be certain . . . ' Op. Cit. p. 162), which imply that when assessing evidences for miracles, we need go no further than to regard candidate evidences as indicating what might just as well be ordinary 'non-miraculous' exceptional phenomena. Ordinarily,

79

however strong may be the body of such candidate evidences, as long as the alleged event is unrepeatable, we cannot as yet take the evidences to be those of a recalcitrance. At any rate, there always could be an explanation which would show the occurrence to be not a recalcitrance. Testimonies, like claims that miracles were sighted, are easily explained in terms of mental delusion. If, say, there were five hundred witnesses, and if it seems improbable that so many can be simultaneously deluded about the same event, then it would be more reasonable to assume this improbability to be overruled rather than the better established scientific law. 'Physical traces' (Swinburne, 1970, p. 34) do indicate an event, but they cannot (since miracles are unrepeatable) be taken as evidences of a recalcitrance. Flew's thesis is strong because, given only the candidate evidences and no other clue, we can in assessing them do nothing besides resorting to the more exact physical sciences for standards of plausibility.

I think, however, that religious contextual considerations could here again provide the basis for a proper defence of miracles. Such a defence must rest on the possibility of situations where the **physical** sciences cannot, even on the Humean criteria, constitute the final arbiter of what is possible and probable. Now, if all we had for evidences were testimonies, then Flew could reply that the religious setting is after all conducive to the having of illusions. But since physical traces indicate an occurrence (although perhaps only an apparently exceptional one), they could give credence to the testimonies; so that the combined weight of physical traces and testimonies would be more than that of physical traces by themselves. Suppose there were numerous occasions within the religious setting when, coinciding with a religiously ideological personality's demonstration of divine power, there were available numerous physical traces and testimonies for the alleged event. Now, if rare occurrences (which physical traces and testimonies can jointly confirm) could within religious contexts be plausibly regarded as miraculous (Cf.pp.76-77), it follows that physical traces and testimonies themselves could, in such situations, be taken as evidences for miracles. At any rate, the repeated coincidence of the availability of the traces and testimonies with the context could by itself render plausible the religious explanation of the evidences. For again, could we conceive of a natural explanation of physical traces of rare phenomena, with collaborating testimonies, repeatedly occurring coincidentally with the activities and intentions of a certain sort of religious personage? Also, could our criteria, governing the acceptance of such coincidences as only ordinary and natural, be met? (Cf. p. 77) And could we still claim to be at a loss for explanations, since it now would seem that religion offers the most plausible one? The improbability of the coincidences being only natural ones would also bolster our regard for other improbabilities (like that of five hundred witnesses being under the same delusion) in the same context - improbabilities which, left on their own, would mean their overruling in favour of scientific plausibility.

It might need the combined weight of, say, an entire tradition of such coincidences occurring in connexion with the activities and intentions of numerous religious personalities to render it just as implausible to doubt the evidences as it is to abandon the scientific law. This conflict, where it can occur, has to be irreconcilable, and not, as Swinburne suggests, a matter of balancing two sets of probabilities. For the less probable the scientific law, the easier it would be to regard the evidences as only those of an ordinary anomaly.

(ii)   The Evidential Value of Miracles and
         Correlated Special Experiences

I shall now suggest how a theistic case might be built on miraculous claims. We shall also see that in the context of the ascertainment of miraculous claims, claims to special purportedly religious experience may too be accorded credence and may therefore bolster the entire case for religion.

The strict coincidence envisaged above of recalcitrances occurring within the sort of religious contexts, while providing a very strong case for explaining them in supernatural terms, need not, it must now be noted, always obtain for the sort of occurrences to be accepted as miraculous. It seems, for instance, that if a sufficient number of fundamental recalcitrances occurred within the context of a religiously ideological personality's life-activities but never quite happening just as he said they would happen, sufficient wonder would already have been generated, for it would already be practically implausible to conceive of a naturalistic explanation for the phenomenon. Thus if Lazarus had not arisen just

81

as Jesus called out to him to arise, but did so some months later, or if he didn't rise at all, but a few others who, let's say, were also called by Jesus to rise from their graves or from their chronic illness did rise even if many days later, the phenomenon as a whole could suffice as being evident for the miraculous. It should also be noted that in the case of recent putative miracles, evidences for which would be fresh and perhaps still existent for cross-checking (e.g. the witnesses could be cross-examined in person, and traces of the recalcitrant occurrences could still be tested), we might be able to decide in favour of the theistic explanation even where the incident occurred only once or twice among our religious personality's life-activities. And viewing a religion as the entire tradition, if the movement stands out as having numerous such exceptional occurrences in the context of the activities of various men of similar religious persuasions down through the ages, more rational weight would be placed on the religious interpretation of the occurrences, for the same reason that the coincidence of the occurrences within the life-activities of numerous personages of the particular religious persuasion might again be difficult to explain naturalistically. (Indeed, in view of the universalistic view of world religions suggested in Part One, similar 'miraculous' occurrences ascertained in other religious traditions could also be brought in to bolster the theistic case).

Our considerations so far show that miracles could conceivably be identified and ascertained. Thus conceptual plausibility has been given to the enterprise of basing theism on miraculous occurrences. Now, it would seem then that in assessing any claim to the miraculous, it won't do to high-handedly dismiss it simply because the experimentally non-repeatable physically impossible is being claimed, even though the fundamental clash, between the scientific plausibility of rejecting miracles and the scientific implausibility of taking the strict coincidence of recalcitrances within the religious contexts to be mere naturalistic phenomena, may be absent.

However, because persisting on this conceptually possible venture would force us to consider claims even of the occurrence of the most fantastic, we may have to require such claims to pass an initial practical plausibility test, before they should be given serious consideration. (We have therefore here a smaller scale parallel to the general requirement,

which we are trying to satisfy, that more than mere
intelligibility of the theistic world view is needed
before it is to be entertained as a serious hypothesis
to truth). The first criterion should be an internally directed one requiring an assessment of the factual purportability of the claim. Obviously, fairy
tales shouldn't be taken as purportedly factual, and
so shouldn't the plainly mythological stories, say of
ancient Greece, about the dealings of gods with men,
told during eras when history and myth were not clearly separated. Whether the purported factuality of
such stories should be seriously regarded would also
depend on their context. The Resurrection, within the
gospel story, would pass as a serious contention
because of its relevance to the religious message,
whereas stories of semi-gods molesting mortal maidens
would not. Now the neo-Humean sort of contention
could be apposite here; for where critical literary
appraisal shows claims to be not really purportedly
factual ones, then a high-handed dismissal of them on
the ground that they are physically impossible, i.e.
obvious fantasies, would be in place. The neo-Humean
error, thus, could be in lumping such cases with those
we conceived above, where a high-handed dismissal of
miracles would be implausible. The second criterion
should require some initial indication of the imminence
of a fundamental clash between scientific plausibility
and the rejection of the miraculous. Thus, even in
the absence of strong features like physical traces,
that show inescapably that a recalcitrance did occur,
as long as there is an initial indication of such a
clash, say, in five hundred witnesses having been re-
liably recorded to have testified to the Ascension, an
initial indication of a possible clash would exist,
assuming it is scientifically implausible for so many
to be deluded about the same thing at the same time.
In other words the test for such initial indicativeness
lies in whether enough evidences are produced to necessitate the abandoning, once the evidences are given a
naturalistic explanation, of certain principles about
good evidences which have all along been regarded as
scientific. Assuming naturalism here would mean dis-
regarding what ordinarily would be taken to be strong
evidences. Of course, by themselves such evidences
(unlike physical traces which show inescapably that a
recalcitrance occurred) could be eventually regarded
as inconclusive, since it is easy to conceive of
principles of good evidences to be overruled by fresh
knowledge such as that following the principles would
lead to the 'absurd' acceptance of evidences for the

'miraculous'. But remembering that ascertaining the miraculous has been shown conceivable, such initial indicativeness would be sufficient to provide initial credibility to the apologetic endeavour and render the contention to be deserving of serious notice. However where there is no such initial indication, then again the neo-Humean thesis would be apposite, for we shouldn't be expected to take seriously any claim (however serious its purport to factuality) to the occurrence of the physically impossible. It is right that we accord different evidential value to the claims of (1) a man who purports that he saw birds in a bird-park ten years ago, though he can't produce any evidence for this besides his testimony, and (2) a man who claims to have seen a lion flying ten years ago in a zoo, but who has only his testimony as evidence. The latter could be high-handedly dismissed, not only because the whole thing lacks factual purportability, but also because nothing is produced to distinguish, at least initially, the claim from those of people who 'see things'. Thus the neo-Humean thesis would be entirely in place as a pragmatic check at this initial stage of the consideration of claims to the miraculous.

A correlated case may be drawn for purported special religious experiences like mystical states, the seeing of visions, and special dreams. Now, there would of course be no physical traces of such events, so that testimonies to such experiences having occurred coincidentally with the intentions and activities of some religious ideological personage could be more easily regarded naturalistically, say as being the out-come of mental suggestion. But once such experiences, together with supporting testimonies, are purported to have occurred in correlation with purported miraculous performances, then the conceivability of miracles (which can have physical traces) being attested would also render it conceivable that the religious explana-tion of those special experiences be rationally com-pelling. For once those miracles, intended say to demonstrate God's power, were ascertained, then certain special experiences, whose outward manifestations could be detected by eye-witnesses (e.g. the state of being in a trance) and which were also purported to be simi-larly intended, would have coincided too well with the context to take a naturalistic explanation. Thus, if say, the Resurrection of Jesus were ascertained, then the appearances of Jesus to the eleven apostles, or even the transfiguration experience early in his minis-try, would be susceptible to explanation in terms of supernatural agency. Now that special religious experiences could, in conjunction with ascertained miracles, be taken as having occurred, it follows, too, that according initial plausibility to the theistic case, once enough collaborating testimonies to special experiences are present in such contexts as that of religious ideological demonstration, would be rational, in at least the sense that a possibility has not been arbitrarily dismissed. Of course, our other criterion of initial practical plausibility in terms of the seriousness of factual pruportability would also apply to the present issue.

After the initial plausibility tests are passed in the ascertaining of miracles and correlated special experiences, must we require of religion the high degree of plausibility, as that arising from the clash between scientific plausibility and the rejection of the miraculous, before we would agree that a basis, significant enough for our purpose, has been provided for the belief in miracles and special religious experiences? I think that if we could produce enough grounds to keep the issue open (i.e. where no definite decision against the theistic viewpoint is, not just logically, but commonsensibly necessitated, even though nothing decisive could be affirmed for theism), the case would be sufficient to render the theistic belief in such events not unreasonable, even from the viewpoint of public rationality. We must bear in mind that the fact that Biblical miracles and special experiences occurred a long time ago (so that whatever the evidences available would be perpetually disputed and physical traces of events would of course be absent) could in some instances be taken as a point in favour of the theistic cause, once initial practical plausibility has been established in the case. For if the case deserves consideration on account of its being initially plausible, then the fact that in the matter one couldn't expect too many evidences because of certain expected limitations accruing from its pastness could render rational the acceptability of the case with less than the usually required evidence. There are similar cases in secular history where a purported long past occurrence is reasonably accepted by decision to be a fact, even though the evidences, on the usual criteria, are theoretically inconclusive; and this is partly because there could never be, in the nature of the case, evidences measuring up to the normal standards. As regards our present case, we have seen that the 'practical impossibility' of the purported occurrences would

make it necessary for us to be more wary of, while not
ruling out, the evidence. But this only shows that
more evidences than usual would be needed for our case
to reach the decision-stage of such cases in secular
history.

I shall now briefly indicate the ways to build
an actual case along the lines suggested. As regards
Biblical claims to miracles and special experiences,
the following sorts of observation, if shown reasonable, could be argued to be sufficient to bring the
theistic case past the stage of initial plausibility.

(1)   Certain documents testifying to the
       miraculous, like the Resurrection,
       or experiences like the transfigura-
       tion of Jesus in the presence of Peter,
       James and John, are either first-hand
       accounts written by eye-witnesses, or
       records of such accounts obtained by
       the writer from the original eye-
       witnesses. Many Bible scholars would
       agree that Luke wrote the gospel
       attributed to him and The Acts; and
       if this were so, then the further
       observation that Luke was at least
       for a span of time a co-worker with
       Paul (Cf. the 'we' passages in The
       Acts), and certainly had associations
       with the original apostles such as
       Peter and James, would allow us the
       reasonable inference that he must
       have checked at least parts of the
       gospel story, and the special and
       miraculous events in The Acts with
       these eye-witnesses. His style had
       been noted to be that of a meticulous
       historian. Also, some of the Pauline
       epistles are widely agreed to be from
       Paul's own pen, and Paul would have
       enough meetings with Peter, James and
       others to have verbal confirmations
       of the stories surrounding the person
       of Jesus which were being told from
       mouth to mouth in the early church.

(2)   On the basis of the above sort of
       information, considerations of the
       following sort could be made. If it
       were so that Biblical writers like

86

> Paul and Luke must have recorded
> what they themselves and also eye-
> witnesses like Peter and James had
> seen and heard, could they all be
> deliberately lying, or could they
> all be deceived or under some kind
> of illusion as regards miracles and
> special experiences? If the expla-
> nation is in terms of delusions,
> could this be adequate to account
> for the sustained recurrences of
> visions and special events, like the
> purported healings of the sick by
> Peter, recorded in The Acts? (A
> very interesting attempt at popular-
> ising such arguments may be found in
> Stott, 1958).

It is clearly conceivable for the sort of
enquiry suggested above to establish at least initial
practical plausibility in favour of belief in the
Biblical miracles and special experiences, for it
could surely provide enough reasons for dismissal of
the theistic case to issue in our having to disregard
certain commonsense psychological assumptions as
regards whether so many could be deluded about the
same things at the same time. Also it is clear that
those special events were being seriously mooted by
the Biblical writers to be facts. And the events
could be plausibly argued to be profoundly significant
for Christianity in precisely the way we are trying to
suggest, i.e. in serving as the basis of a case for
theism.

Apart from Biblical special events, other
purported miracles and special experiences within the
entire religious tradition (and in other religious
traditions too, given our case for religious universalism in Part One) could conceivably be similarly considered; for it is at least conceivable for eye-witness
accounts and perhaps even physical traces (in the case
of recent putative miracles) to be available. Now,
viewing the religious tradition (or the universal tradition of religions) as a whole, even if all the credibility we could establish for putative miracles and
special experiences were only initial practical plausibility for a sufficient number of incidents, we
would have provided significant grounds for the theistic contention; for the coincidence of so many such
cases where the initial plausibility is attained within

a common (or basically common) religious ideological framework would already be a cause for wonder. This would apply too where so many such purported occurrences take place in the context of the activities and intentions of individual religious personages. And where we have a religious tradition (or a tradition of religions) in which lived a sufficient number of such religious personages, whose lives are wonder-inspiring in this way, the coincidence of all these within a similar (or basically similar) religious ideological framework could itself be too great a 'miracle' to be explained naturalistically. It would be hard to explain naturalistically how, within the context of similar religious intentions and practices, so many of our normal assumptions about psychology and good evidences would have to be so repetitively abandoned. I think at some such points, the sceptic should rationally cease, and begin to entertain the religious proposition as at least worthy of consideration.

I have in the above paragraph proposed only tentatively, within brackets, that the backdrop of a similar religious persuasion, wherein the envisaged coincidence of miraculous and special occurrences would be significant, might be a universal phenomenon cutting across the major religious traditions. The tentativeness is due to my being aware, not only that the question of religious universalism is highly contentious, but that for apologetic purposes the universal backdrop may be too diffused for granting the envisaged coincidental special occurrences the wonderment mentioned. To one not yet about to be convinced, it might seem far-fetched that a miracle in the near east could have any significant connection with another in China, even granting the basic similarity of world religions. So for our apologetic purpose, it might be better to establish our case with reference to one religious context, and leave the question of universalism to arise only after the rationality of at least one religion has been established. Then, similar special occurrences in other religions, along with a good argument for religious universalism, could be solicited to bolster the case further.

Now, how does belief in miracles and special experiences bolster religion? Here we must mention briefly and refute Alasdair MacIntyre's widely acknowledged paper 'The Logical Status of Religious Beliefs' (MacIntyre, 1957), especially the part which concerns the appropriateness and feasibility of the apologetic

use of putative miracles. (pp. 206-211) On the general fideistic position of the essay,* we need only
observe that it confuses religious adherence with
religious discourse. Even if religious adherents
believe in religion in the manner described by MacIntyre and regard evidences as irrelevant to belief,
this should not prevent others or even the fideist himself from participating in the discourse of examining
grounds for belief. Some others might need independent
evidences before accepting even fideism. In the
fideist's case, surely he could participate in the
reasoning about evidences to settle his intellectual
curiosity even though the outcome of that would have
no effect on his religious commitments. And there
surely exist other sorts of religious adherents whose
religious commitment would be affected by the outcome
of religious thinking; at any rate such religious
adherents could exist, and any comprehensive descriptive analysis of the logical status of religious beliefs should surely also consider possible religious
stances.

But of more interest to us is what seems to be
MacIntyre's prescriptive thesis that since everything
of importance to religions is outside the reach of
historical investigation we might as well accept his
analysis of the nature of religious beliefs. He illustrates this by observing, with regard to the Resurrection, that (1) because the rift in belief about this
goes back to the earliest testifiers, it would be
impossible to base a judgement about the matter on
purported evidences, and (2) even if historians could
decide that the event had occurred, the decision would
regard only the rising of Jesus from the dead, from
which fact alone it would be unwarranted to infer an
act of God. MacIntyre, to illustrate the first point,
describes an imaginary assessment of documents certi-
fied by Ciaiphas or the apostles alleging the genuine-

---

* MacIntyre's view should not be confused with the reductionistic theses mentioned in our Introduction (Cf. pp.x-xi).
The fideism of MacIntyre isn't the outcome of denying the very
truth-claims that call for evidences. The truth-claims are
indeed acknowledged, but regarded as being in no need for proof.

ness or otherwise of the Resurrection. Believers and non-believers alike could accept the 'evidence' that seems favourable to their contention, and take that which seems unfavourable as another piece of Christian or anti-Christian fabrication.

Now, granted that the dispute about the Resurrection goes back to the earliest testifiers, the resulting difficulties in the assessment of the documents are not logical but merely practical ones, which are in principle surmountable. As regards MacIntyre's imagined documents, if there are no other such documents that might directly help to decide for or against the theistic position, the historian might be able indirectly to, say, detect traits of character of the author from other documents in order to determine whether such a personality could have fabricated the case, or could have been deceived or mad. The answer, even if not decisive, could give more rational weight to one position or the other. Even when evidences are too scarce for any such determination, MacIntyre's imaginary documents could be evidence enough to cause a question-mark to hover over the issue. And we have said that more recent putative miracles within a similar religious tradition could more conceivably be shown to have occurred, since less disputed documents would be more readily available. Such miracles, once confirmed, could bolster our regard for the Biblical miracles. The upshot is that we need not as yet be discouraged by MacIntyre from our apologetic pursuit.

Regarding MacIntyre's second point we should first observe that even if it is true that historical inquiry could only settle the question about, say, the rising of Jesus from the dead, it does not follow that the enquiry has absolutely no bearing on the rationality or otherwise of the belief about an act of God. MacIntyre has himself noted that although the Resurrection involves more than the physical rising of Jesus from the dead, the latter is necessarily a component of it. At any rate, the feat of Jesus' rising to life after having been dead three days, viewed in the light of his claims and teachings, and his predictions about the very act itself as the supreme demonstration of his 'divinity', all this considered with his other miracles (assuming these were also ascertained), would at least establish him as an extra-ordinary, nay, supernatural person whose teachings and claims are not to be lightly dismissed.

But the method I propose for ascertaining special religious events would have, if successfully deployed, implicated an act of God in its conclusions. Let us recall the situations of coincidence of evidences and fundamental recalcitrances to natural laws occurring within certain religious contexts on which basis we have argued that miracles and special religious experiences could be confirmed. Now the context of explanation of the coincidences is a religious one where God is conceived at least as the conscious agent of miracles and special experiences. Could one go as far as accepting supernatural agency for the acts and yet deny that God, in some minimal sense, is that agent? After all, such is the agency whose power is being demonstrated by the sort of religious protagonists within whose apologetic efforts the coincidences are envisaged to have occurred. Of course not everything said within the religious tradition about this God need be accepted, but at least conscious agency and power over nature, which seem implied by the intentionality of the coincidental situations referred to, should be conceded to.

Once God, in this minimal sense, is reasonably accepted as existing, then surely a strong contention for the acceptability of the religious tradition within which he features (and even basically similar traditions elsewhere) is provided. We need remind ourselves again that no proofs in the ordinary sense can be given for religion, given the logic of religious discourse. To this extent is fideism true, for though reasons for religious beliefs must be given, a leap of thought, as we said before, is still required somewhere along the line. Our contention therefore is that given a religious tradition within which belief in a sufficient number of miracles is made reasonable, together with belief in certain special experiences, sufficient grounds would already exist to render theism rationally reputable.

The theistic conclusions thus arrived at would not commit what T.R. Miles (Miles, 1972, pp. 29-31) has called 'the absolute-existence mistake'. Taking God's existence to be like that of 'a man in the top flat' does not in our case involve a basic linguistic shift; for we have grounds for the theistic postulate. The intentionality detectable in our envisaged situations of the coincidences is explicable only in terms of supernatural agency. Now the intentionality and the intervention with the natural order are ascribable only to conscious agency, similar to our man in the top flat in at least this fundamental respect. In our envisaged situations, this 'God' would seem, too, to share the evangelical zeal of the human religious protagonists concerned as regards some at least of the theological beliefs which the particular religious tradition has established. So if the tradition describes God in anthropomorphic terms, then we have more reasons to warrant the analogy between God and a human person. The linguistic shift involved in the way we substantiate the concept of God might occur only where we postulate an incorporeal, omnipotent, omniscient, timeless, immutable (and so on) deity on only the basis of our having established a conscious, supernatural and personal agent. But once we reasonably believe in an unseen and supernatural manipulator of things, then we are already well on the way to accepting a substantive part of what the tradition (whose religious beliefs are upheld by such an agent through the performance of miracles) would teach about God. (These considerations, be it noted, provide us with a substantive experiential basis for giving sense to the concept of incorporeal, transcendent personhood as applied to God; which is a point we merely anticipated in our discussions in Part One of the conceptual difficulties of theism, Cf. pp. 27-33).

Two possible objections to our contention remain to be considered. Firstly, it might be urged that providing grounds for theism would be against the logic of the _unconditional_ adherence to religious truths required by religions, so that it would not be authentic theism that is supported by our case. Secondly, it might be said that, far from there being independent grounds facilitating the leap of faith that is necessary for the acceptance of religion despite conceptual difficulties like that of evil, the latter fundamental logical difficulties would render suspect any independent putative grounds for theism.

It may be urged, with regard to the first objection, that the unconditional belief which theism requires is already adequately accounted for in our contention that experiential grounds could be laid to render reasonable the theistic leap of faith. Surely the leap is to the regions of _unconditional_ belief, in the sense that, provided the minimal intelligibility condition is met (Cf. pp. 2 - 3), no conceptual difficulties as regards doctrines or any other questions _apart from the questioning of the experiential grounds_ themselves could conceivably destroy the faith. For such conceptual difficulties that remain (expectedly) of religious beliefs, after initial indications of good sense have been established for them, could, with religion grounded on independent evidences, be consistently shelved provisionally as divine mystery, which is a defining attribute of the deity. As regards the grounds themselves for the leap of faith, it is clear that grounds by definition are conditional, so that once grounds are admitted to be necessary for religious belief, it is the philosopher's job to clarify that religion has implicitly agreed to the conditionality of such grounds. And didn't the early apostles base their preachings on the putative fact of the risen Christ, seen of them during a period of some forty days and nights, and of the Ascension? (These were the events that brought them back from despair and disillusionment). Haven't believers, who perhaps had made the leap of faith even without having been given real grounds (say after a Billy Graham rally), denounced the faith after, say, a philosophy course? Hadn't theologians tried to prove the existence of God? My analysis of a grounded belief, I think, accounts for both the unconditionality of religious belief and the fact that philosophic disproofs of religion have affected at least sophisticated believers. The latter are those who are better able to appreciate the point of religious discourse, and whose enlightened position should therefore be taken as the best representation of religious belief.

The second sort of objection was raised by Antony Flew against Aquinas' conviction that the metaphysician can prove the existence of God independently of the problem of evil, and so we must assume there is a solution to the problem even though it hasn't as yet been given. Flew opined that as long as the notion of God's existing cannot accommodate apparently falsifying facts, it remains a possibility that any ostensible proofs for theism are at fault. (Flew,1966, pp. 58-59). But Flew's position hinges on the erroneous view that the sort of conceptual difficulties would remain even where theism is reasonably believed in on proper grounds. Since mystery is inherent in the concept of God, where such grounds exist for religious belief, any such difficulties, provided the religious beliefs satisfy the minimal intelligibility condition, could be consistently shelved in the mystery section. (It could be that the proviso just stressed would suffice to compromise Aquinas' and Flew's positions).

(iii)   Rational Personal Belief

So far, we have only been concerned with showing that <u>public</u> rational grounds for religion of the kind indicated are conceivable, and practically possible to obtain. It may be unlikely that fresh evidences for the Biblical miracles and other special events to add to what supporting documents are presently available will ever be had. Admittedly the available documents are inconclusive, despite our above indications of the evidential value they provide. However, the theistic case envisaged still remains a practical possibility, since if past purported miracles and special experiences cannot be conclusively ascertained, a spate of such occurrences might crop up in the future under circumstances that may warrant the religious conclusions. Should this occur, then, as we said, other less well-evidenced special events of the past would be also evidenced, and collectively a case for theism would be had. Now, this may seem a pious hope, but I think the <u>conceivability</u> of the practical possibility being realised has practical import in the more esoteric arena of personal religious conviction, even if in itself it seems likely to remain of mere theoretical interest. We will elaborate on this practical import in a moment. Now it must be further observed that in fact the logic of <u>miracles</u> and other <u>special</u> events may be such as not to warrant the expectation that such events can occur readily and often enough for some selected few of them to be picked ('few', because of the expectedly <u>rare</u> presence of available publicly ascertainable supporting evidences) to be the basis of a public rational theistic case. Even in the life-time of Jesus, only a few lepers or the dead were miraculously healed or raised to life, out of the multitudes of lepers and the dead there must have been. Anyhow, miracles are rare by definition, and special experiences are of course <u>special</u>. The apologetic use of such special religious events (a use which was clearly intended, at least in apostolic Christianity) may never, in the nature of things, have been meant for producing a theistic case in the arena of <u>public</u> rationality. Rather, it could be meant for a case in the personal and more or less esoteric arena of individual conviction, a use of miracles and special experiences that is possible, as we shall show, only after it is shown conceptually and practically possible in the arena of public rationality. And the logic of religious response may require,

94

as we mentioned in Part One (p. 38), that no conclusive
or compelling public grounds exist for belief, since
the existential conditions of human life could be such
that once God's existence were proven, man's cognisance of this would also determine his religious response. Men are not devils who can 'believe and yet
tremble' rather than respond. In order to retain the
freedom to respond or not in the religious quest, it
could be that some kind of initiation - where some
evidence of the more personal kind, supported, in the
way we shall indicate, by initial public rational considerations, along with other more subjective willingness and initiative to 'ask' and 'seek' and 'knock',
leading by degrees to the initiate's being 'given' and
'finding' and to doors being opened to him, depending
on such preparedness as some volitional initiative
first being shown - may be necessary. This fine tem-
pering and juxtaposing of esoterism and faith with
reason, beginning at the more public stages, but leading on to more esoteric 'seeings' which the non-ini-
tiate necessarily cannot appreciate, culminating
perhaps at what might be dramatically called 'an encounter with the deity', may be the unique 'verification' procedures appropriate to knowledge of the transcendent and holy. I say 'may', for again, in the logic
of things, I can't prove it. If I could, people would
be compelled to try it. Rational respectability and
possibility could be all that can be indicated, and all
are invited to take the reasonable initiative to come
and 'taste that the Lord is good'. Thus to preserve
man's autonomy, it could be that the search for God has
necessarily to be in crucial parts a vertical approach,
though not totally unsupported by horizontal discursive
thinking; and crucial vertical leaps of thought pro-
pelled by the willingness and initiative of a free
response, that is not valueless for being careless and
unreasonable, tempered as it is by horizontal, discursive reasoning, could be absolutely essential if God
is to reveal himself through meeting man half-way and
thus do so in a manner not destructive of man's autonomy. The revelation would of course be absolutely
crucial if man is ever to know of the transcendent -
the necessary limitations of human experience and
language, and thus of discursive reasoning based on
those, for the search of divine truths if these exist,
have all been stressed before. But if revelation is
not to disrupt man's autonomy, the half-way house
suggested above, where God can meet man who has reached there by his own initiative among other things,
could be essential.

Now this vertical-cum-horizontal religious enquiry, leading ultimately to a revelatory disclosure, or intuition or a leap of thought, seems to be what H.D. Lewis, Gibson, Owens and Hick have, in their several ways discussed in Section I, tried inadequately to intimate. As I mentioned, they have only succeeded in drawing our attention, as far as their discursive and horizontal reasonings go, to the features of the natural world or our natural experience that tally with the theistic postulate of creative orderliness; we saw that these features, by themselves and unsupported by more telling discursive considerations, could not, at least from the standpoint of public rationality, render rationally reputable the claimed intuition, disclosure or leap of thought, however authentic and religiously significant these in truth may be. Now how has our above case based on miracles and other special events provided the missing foundation for mooting these accounts of religious experience and evidence as rationally reputable?

Now if miracles and special religious experiences are intelligible and their ascertainment practically possible in the manner indicated, then it is conceivable and practically possible that some at least of the traditional claims to miracles and special experiences could have been true, except that because of their pastness or of deficiencies in documentation or the lack of eye-witnesses, etc., the clash of probabilities occasioned by the envisaged coincidence of evidences and context does not exist for their ascertainment on the criteria of public rationality. This weakly evidenced possibility of their being true, although in normal contexts might not be positive enough to warrant serious attention, would in the context of religious claims - where there could occur numerous incidents, in believers' personal lives, of religiously significant 'miraculous' coincidences of events analogous in form to our envisaged occasions of publicly ascertained miracles - be significant enough to warrant its being seriously entertained. This will be explained and argued for below. Anyhow (1) the pastness of the Biblical events, for which evidences must necessarily be too inconclusive for the rigorous case for miracles we envisaged (we said this should warrant the acceptability of the truth-claim on less rigorous grounds, p. 85); (2) the point that if there were a publicly attested proof of miracles, and therefore of religious truth-claims, human free choice for God would be undermined; (3) our contention that the fact that the cosmos and human experience are such as to be amenable to theistic explanation already contains some evidential value for theism; and (4) our point that the fact that miracles and other special events are sensible and testable already contains some evidential value: all these points must combine, together with whatever textual and testimonial evidences are presently available for the Biblical special events, to provide the conceptual and public evidential backdrop necessary for an intelligent enquirer to proceed to test religious truth-claims in his own life. This is especially so in a religious tradition wherein multitudes of the faithful have testified to having successfully tested them in their own lives.

It is worth noting at this stage that this contention, for the possibility of Biblical miracles and other special events being true and confirmable in the more esoteric realm of personal experience, is _in practice_ unfalsifiable, even though in principle falsifiable. In practice, no new documents other than what are available can be envisaged which would decisively count against it. We have the testimonies of the Gospels, the Acts and some epistles and their evidential value, considered on public criteria, for what they are worth. Either a rational decision in favour of them, in part grounded in personal evidences, is made; or the issue should be left open. There can be no other alternative in the matter of the case. This partly explains, surely, the dogmatism of religious belief; although grounds are appealed to, which we said imply falsifiability (Cf. p. 93), in practice believers live their religious lives as if nothing would falsify their beliefs. Indeed no hard evidences would, if their beliefs were grounded at rock bottom on Biblical miracles; although in the area of personal rational decisions they still may abandon the faith, like some have. (These comments serve to qualify our observations made above on the falsifiability but also unconditionality of religious belief, pp. 92 - 93).

Now against the conceptual and evidential backdrop indicated have arisen numerous personal claims and testimonies to events and experiences in believers' personal lives, which are insisted on more or less esoteric grounds to be 'miraculous' and religiously significant. Some are claimed to be more public, like the visions at Lourdes and the connected traditions of healing experiences that arose thereafter. Others occur more in autobiographies, with their authors affirming conviction that certain events or patterns of events were for themselves personal 'encounters' with the deity even though no claim were made that they would meet with public rational criteria. Many of these are established church literature, like St. Augustine's Confessions, while it is indeed common for the most ordinary believers at devotional services to testify to occasions in their lives where interpretations in terms of divine manifestations seem inescapable, subjectively considered. Now I think the fact that, considered on public criteria, such coincidental circumstances, as envisaged in Section II (i) and (ii) above, do warrant belief in miracles (and indeed are somewhat obtained in the case of Biblical miracles) would provide rational weight for belief in these more personal miraculous claims if analogous coincidental events and experiences were the bases of them. For although they in themselves seem insufficiently evidenced, they set a pattern of real possibilities which could well be repetitively enacted in the form of events in numerous personal lives within a whole tradition. Thus if on numerous occasions in my life experiences, things prayed for seemed to have happened soon after prayer, and this is also startlingly observed by my fellow-participants in prayer-meetings in their own life-experiences, the envisaged pattern of miraculous coincidences would seem to have been repeatedly re-enacted, and the coincidence of this, and indeed of the entire tradition of such common experiences of believers, with the undoubtedly but expectedly weakly documented coincidental patterns of Biblical special events, must suffice to generate some wonder. And the crucial element in the personal leaps of thought or faith made in such 'encounter' experiences must be the expected esoteric 'vertically directed' ingredient that is juxtaposed with such 'horizontal' discursive considerations. These confirmatory assurances further coincide with such recognition of religious significance in such coincidental events, and only the initiate (who knows?), who has begun to seek, perhaps even to pray such prayers as 'God if you exist, please reveal', might receive them.

It may seem that my attempt to delineate the basis of personal religious conviction is not much different from Lewis', Gibson's or Owens', which I said earlier are insufficient. The difference however is this. Whereas from the viewpoint of personal belief it may be true that Lewis' delineation of religious experience, say, is significant enough in its drawing attention to ordinary features and events, yet from the viewpoint of public rationality, unless the sort of coincidences we envisaged is somewhat replicated even in the more esoteric realm of personal experience, there could be no warrant to resort to religious, non-naturalistic explanations. Indeed, because of the innate esoterism of such claims, no publicly conclusive theistic case would arise from the personal case. This we said is necessary for human autonomy of response, if religion were true. But because of its _formal_ acceptability; and also the evidential value arising from the coinciding of such personal replicas of the miraculous coincidences of events in the entire reli-gious context; and the enhanced evidential value the central Biblical special events surely in turn enjoy, with their credibility supported somewhat by the re-peated replication of their pattern of coincidental events in the personal context of belief: it would I think be unduly high-handed and untrue to the dictates of unbiased truth-enquiry if the personal leaps of thought or faith that result be not accorded enough respect to allow for their authenticity to be at least respected as an open issue on public criteria. After all, the said coincidence of events in the believer's private experience, although not comprising hard public evidences, would be similar in form and therefore _continuous in kind_ to the hard public grounds for miracles we envisaged. The possibility must therefore be left open that what is lacking in public evidences to clinch the case for publicly purported miracles may in the area of personal experiential evidences be remedied through, say, divine disclosures and confir-mation coinciding with wonderfully coinciding personal events. And because these disclosures are esoteric, and expectedly so in the nature of religion, the outside rational observer would be ill-qualified to pass judge-ment on them. All in, we have a cumulative case to allow for the possibility of the personal case for re-ligion being true.

III CONCLUDING REMARKS: RELIGIOUS INSTRUCTION IN
     A LIBERAL EDUCATION

On public rational criteria, there is, as we have shown, an intelligible and practically possible way to ascertain religious truth-claims. Indeed there are available some, although insufficient, positive public evidences of the sort envisaged. In practice, it may seem unlikely that sufficient public evidences would be available to affirm theism. This is not to say that the issue is to be left in practice perpetually open. We have also argued that the confirmation of religious truths may conceivably and quite reputably be effected in the arena of personal grounds and conviction - which is just the sort of verification religion would require if human autonomy _visavis_ God is to be preserved. With religious truths confirmed on such grounds, then, as we argued in Part One, the suspension of disbelief, enabled by our partial explanations there of evil,should surely give way to faith that those indicators available in the human experience as to satisfactory cosmic and divine explanations of evil do indeed indicate a satisfactory ultimate explanation. Apart from the problem of evil, the other conceptual problems of the defining attributes of God, which we didn't regard as serious enough to discuss as fully, should pose no real difficulty to the faith in religion now shown reputable. Our way of basing belief on the coincidence of events in certain contexts, which can only be reasonably explained in terms of miraculous supernatural intervention by an agent the context ideologically identifies as God, would also, as we pointed out, be the basis of the intelligibility of the postulate of incorporeal and transcendent personhood and agency. Compared to this central theistic notion, and to the problem of evil and the crucial defining attributes of God (which, we argued, are not really problematic; (Cf.pp.12-14)), other traditional conceptual difficulties that remain must be peripheral and of no real consequence to basic belief. Also in the event of the discovery of extraterrestrial biological persons (and we said that divine plan and creativity would be called in question if such persons didn't exist,p. 15), our remedy in Part One, in terms of an universalist religious reinterpretation, for the continued intelligibility of world religions despite that discovery (p.25), would be the more rationally compelling in view of our case in this part for the possible reasonableness of religious belief.

Therefore from the viewpoint of the enhancement of knowledge and understanding in a liberal education, we ignore the real possibility of a unique religious dimension of knowledge at our peril. This is the more so bearing in mind that, if religion were true, then not only would religious knowledge be the kind of knowledge with real permanent value (in the after life, presumably all aposteriori this-worldly forms of knowledge, which are essentially conjectural, as Popper has taught us, would give way to at least greater perfection - 'now we see through a glass darkly, but then face to face'; the physical sciences would especially be outdated with 'a new heaven and a new earth'!); but religious truths, as we noted before, would be the backdrop for understanding the ultimate source or foundation of all secular forms of knowledge. For instance, the 'link' traditionally sought after, and ridiculed by empiricists as 'metaphysical', to connect cause and effect, and to justify induction in the physical sciences would be found in divine institution and consistency if religion were true.

We should therefore teach religion in a liberal curriculum as a viable explanatory possibility, like the way we teach interesting scientific hypotheses. The difference in verification procedures, dictated possibly by the logic of religion itself, in the confirmation of the religious hypothesis, crucially in the individual's own experience and initiation, should be communicated to students, possibly through the discussion of auto-biographies, biographies, and personal oral testimonies. Despite our arguments for a universalistic interpretation of world religions, it may be that a multi-religious approach (subject to a compulsory assertion of a minimal theism, which our mode of testing religious truth-claims would entail and also the religious universalism we advocated would require, (Cf. pp.4-5)), with adherents of different faiths being invited in to supplement the academic teaching of comparative religions with personal invitations given to students to test their faiths in an appropriate theistic sense in their own lives, should be adopted. For a syncretisation of different religions would be another religion itself, and would lack the experience and feel of a tradition of partially public but crucially esoteric insights so necessary to the personal leap of faith we tried to advocate as reputable. Also, our case for a religious universalism is compatible with, indeed involves, in its upholding of a minimal theism, the view that though all religions represent facets of one truth, some may be more perfect than others as manifestations of the truth, depending on the readiness of the peoples concerned for divine revelation. Thus christians might maintain that in Christ, 'God became man' in the most perfect, even 'unique' revelatory act, while still conceding that other religions, even extraterrestial ones, have been attempts, partially achieved, of a similar revelation. Even as fundamentalist a christian writer as C.S. Lewis has maintained some such view. It might therefore be that a syncretisation of religions may be further from the truth than some one or another of actual world religions.* Our religious universalism, however, would justify the tolerance of admitting diverse reputable religions to feature somewhat in the liberal curriculum. Problems normally met in religious education in a religiously plural society, such as parents insisting on their children studying only their own religion, would of course be somewhat alleviated. In this example, as long as such parents' own religions satisfy certain criteria of reputableness (and not, for example, fanatical sects and cults off the main traditions, which would not satisfy the criteria of serious religious hypotheses), studying them to the exclusion of other religions, subject to the proviso that a personal deity is somewhat advocated, would not be too disastrous, since it would be one facet of the same truth that is concerned. Of course these are mere beginnings on the religious quest, for if I am right about the universalism, a convinced believer should eventually be brought to the cosmic understanding, and see his own faith as part of the greater, universal tapestry.

---

* We said when arguing for religious universalism (p. 4) that doctrinal differences among religions, provided a minimal theism is asserted, cannot be significant enough to warrant religious schism since the best religion must still be very imperfect in view of the necessary limitations of the human perspective. But this does not mean that degrees of worldly perfection, once the universalism is acceded to, should not be pursued. Religious differences are indeed significant in terms of the careful striving for perfection which religious adherence enjoins.

SELECT BIBLIOGRAPHY

The papers and books listed below are those referred to in the text, where they are cited by the author's surname and the year of publication, and, where more than one work in the same year by the author are mentioned, also by a letter of the alphabet.

BRAITHWAITE R.B. (1971)   'An Empiricist's View of the Nature of Religious Belief' reprinted in The Philosophy of Religion, Basil Mitchell ed.,London, Oxford University Press

CLARKE, J.J. (1971)   'John Hick's Resurrection' Sophia, Vol. X No. 3

EWING, A.C. (1973)   Value and Reality, London, George Allen and Unwin

FINLAY, J.N. (1955)   'Can God's Existence be Disproved?' in New Essays in Philosophical Theology, Antony Flew and Alasdair MacIntyre ed., London, SCM Press

FLEW, ANTONY (1955)   'Divine Omnipotence and Human Freedom' in New Essays in Philosophical Theology, Antony Flew and Alasdair MacIntyre ed., London, SCM Press

Flew, ANTONY (1961)   Hume's Philosophy of Belief, London, Hutchinson

FLEW, ANTONY (1966)   God and Philosophy, London Macmillan

FLEW, ANTONY (1967)   'Miracles' in Encyclopedia of Philosophy, Vol. 5, Paul Edwards ed., N.Y. and London, Macmillan and The Free Press

FLEW, ANTONY (1973)   'Compatibilism, Freewill and God' _Philosophy_, Vol. 48

GALLIE, W.B. (1964)   _Philosophy and the Historical Understanding_, London, Chatto and Windus

GIBSON, A. BOYCE (1970)   _Theism and Empiricism_, London, SCM Press

HARE, R.M. (1971)   'Theology and Falsification' reprinted in _The Philosophy of Religion_, Basil Mitchell ed., London, Oxford University Press

HICK, JOHN (1957)   _Faith and Knowledge_, Ithaca, Cornell University Press

HICK, JOHN (1963)   _The Philosophy of Religion_ N.J., Prentice Hall; Englewood Cliffs

HICK, JOHN (1969)   'Religious Faith as Experiencing-as' in _Talk of God: Royal Institute of Philosophy Lectures_, Vol. 2, London, Macmillan

HICK, JOHN (1966)   _Evil and the God of Love_, London, Macmillan

HICK, JOHN (1970)   _Arguments for the Existence of God_, London, Macmillan

HICK, JOHN (1972)   'Mr Clarke's Resurrection Also' _Sophia_, Vol. XI, No. 3

HICK, JOHN (1973)   _God and the Universe of Faiths_, London, Macmillan

HICK, JOHN (1976)   _Death and Eternal Life_, London, Collins

HIRST, PAUL H. (1974)   _Knowledge and the Curriculum_, London, Routledge & Kegan Paul

HOLLAND, R.F. (1967)   'The Miraculous' in <u>Relig-
ion and Understanding</u>, D.Z.
Phillips ed. London, Ox-
ford: Blackwell

JAMES, WILLIAM (1941)   <u>The Varieties of Religious
Experience</u>, London, Long-
mans Green (reprint)

LEWIS, C.S. (1940)   <u>The Problem of Pain</u>, Lon-
don, Collins Fontana Books

LEWIS, C.S. (1960)   <u>Miracles</u>, London,Collins
Fontana Books

LEWIS, H.D. (1959)   <u>Our Experience of God</u>, Lon-
don, George Allen and Unwin

LEWIS, H.D. (1973)   <u>The Self and Immortality</u>,
London, Macmillan

MACINTYRE, ALASDAIR(1957)   'The Logical Status of
Religious Beliefs' in <u>Meta-
physical Beliefs</u> Stephen
Toulmin ed., London, SCM
Press

MACINTYRE, ALASDAIR(1968)   'Review of R. Puccetti's
<u>Persons</u>' in <u>The Manchester
Guardian</u>, 6th December

MACKIE, J.L. (1971)   'Evil and Omnipotence'
reprinted in <u>The Philosophy
of Religion</u>, Basil Mitchell
ed., London, Oxford Univer-
sity Press

MILES, T.R. (1959)   <u>Religion and the Scientific
Outlook</u>, London, George
Allen and Unwin

MILES, T.R. (1972)   <u>Religious Experience</u>,London,
Macmillan

NIELSEN, KAI (1971)   <u>Contemporary Critiques of
Religion</u>, London, Macmillan

OTTO, RUDOLF (1932)   <u>Mysticism East and West</u>, New York, Macmillan

OWENS, H.P. (1969)   <u>The Christian Knowledge of God</u>, London, The Athlone Press

PALUCH, STANLEY (1973)   'A Cosmomorphic Utopia', <u>The Personalist</u>, Vol. LV, Winter

PALUCH, STANLEY (1976)   'Tan Tai Wei's Cosmomorphic Utopias' <u>The Personalist</u>, Vol. LVII, Autumn

PETERS, R.S. (1966)   <u>Ethics and Education</u>,London, George Allen and Unwin

PETERS, R.S. (1973a)   'The Justification of Education' in <u>The Philosophy of Education</u> R.S. Peters ed., London, Oxford University Press

PETERS, R.S. (1973b)   <u>Reason and Compassion</u>,London, Routledge and Kegan Paul

PHENIX, P.H. (1964)   <u>Realms of Meaning</u>, New York, McGraw-Hill

PHILLIPS, D.Z. (1965)   <u>The Concept of Prayer</u>, London, Routledge and Kegan Paul

PIKE, NELSON (1970)   <u>God and Timelessness</u>,London, Routledge and Kegan Paul

PRICE, H.H. (1972)   <u>Essays in the Philosophy of Religion</u>, London, Oxford University Press

PUCCETTI, ROLAND (1964)   'The Concept of God '<u>The Philosophical Quarterly</u>, Vol. 14 No. 56, July

PUCCETTI, ROLAND (1967)   'The Loving God - Some Observations of J. Hick's <u>Evil and the God of Love</u>' <u>Religious Studies</u>, Vol. 2

PUCCETTI, ROLAND (1968)   <u>Persons</u>, London, Macmillan

QUINTON, ANTHONY (1973)   The Nature of Things, London, Routledge and Kegan Paul

SMART, NINIAN (1961a)   'The Uncertainty Principle in Religion' The Listener, LXVI

SMART, NINAN (1961b)   'Omnipotence, Evil and Supermen' Philosophy 1961

SMART, NINIAN (1964)   Philosophers and Religious Truth, London, SCM Press

STOTT, JOHN (1958)   Basic Christianity, London, IVF Press

SWINBURNE, RICHARD (1968)   'Miracles' The Philosophical Quarterly, October

SWINBURNE, RICHARD (1970)   The Concept of Miracles, London, Macmillan

TAN TAI WEI (1974)   'The Question of a Cosmomorphic Utopia' The Personalist Vol. 55, No. 4

TAN TAI WEI (1978)   The Concept of Education, Educational Conceptions and Liberal Education, Washington D.C., University Press of America

WALLACE, R.C. (1969)   'Review of R. Puccetti's Persons' The Philosophical Quarterly, October

WALLACE, R.C. (1970)   'Hume, Flew and the Miraculous' The Philosophical Quarterly, July

WINCH, PETER (1977)   'Meaning and Religious Language' in Reason and Religion Stuart C. Brown ed., Ithaca and London, Cornell University Press

WILSON, JOHN (1971)   Education in Religion and the Emotions, London, Heinemann

INDEX

The Problem of Evil:

Transnatural and Incorporeal Personhood and States:

ABOUT THE AUTHOR

Tan Tai Wei was born in Singapore in 1942 and received his education in Singapore, completing his BA (Hons) in Philosophy and English in 1965, and his MA in Philosophy in 1968 in the then University of Singapore. He taught secondary school from 1968 to 1974, during which period he wrote, in 1970, Our Social Framework and its Ethical Basis, a pre-university level reader published and circulated in Singapore. He then published, between 1971 and 1976, eight philosophical papers and discussions in Sophia, Religious Studies, The Personalist, Educational Philosophy and Theory, and The Philosophical Journal. He joined the Institute of Education, Singapore, in 1974, in which he has been responsible for the teaching of the philosophy of education. He has also tutored and lectured part-time in philosophy in the University of Singapore.

His previous book published by University Press of America is The Concept of Education, Educational Conceptions and Liberal Education (1978), a critique of contemporary conceptual analyses and justifications of education which also provides a conceptual framework within which confusions detected in the recent works are resolved and educational discourse properly understood. About it, Antony Flew wrote:

> 'I read this packed and strenuous little book with great pleasure and almost total agreement. He must have established a new record by concentrating so much sound argument into so short a book in the philosophy of education.'

He is married and they have two children.